Susan D. Toliver

Black Families in Corporate America

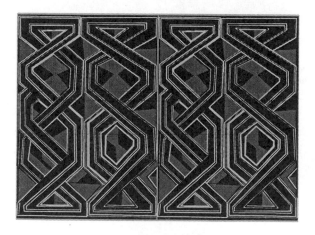

UNDERSTANDING
FAMILIES

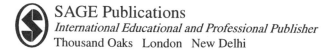
SAGE Publications
International Educational and Professional Publisher
Thousand Oaks London New Delhi

For information:

SAGE Publications, Inc.
2455 Teller Road
Thousand Oaks, California 91320
E-mail: order@sagepub.com

SAGE Publications Ltd.
6 Bonhill Street
London EC2A 4PU
United Kingdom

SAGE Publications India Pvt. Ltd.
M-32 Market
Greater Kailash I
New Delhi 110 048 India

Printed in the United States of America

Library of Congress Cataloging-in-Publication Data

Toliver, Susan Diane.
    Black families in corporate America / by Susan D. Toliver.
        p.   cm.—(Understanding families; v. 11)
    Includes bibliographical references and index.
    ISBN 0-7619-0291-0 (cloth: acid-free paper).—ISBN 0-7619-0292-9
(pbk.: acid-free paper)
        1. Families, Black—United States. 2. Afro-American families.
    3. Middle class families—United States. 4. Work and family—United States.
    5. Corporate culture—United States. I. Title. II. Series.
    HQ536.T55 1998
    306.85′089′96073—dc21   97-33894

98 99 00 01 02 03 10 9 8 7 6 5 4 3 2 1

Acquiring Editor: Jim Nageotte
Editorial Assistant: Fiona Lyon
Production Editor: Diana E. Axelsen
Production Assistant: Lynn Miyata
Typesetter: Rebecca Evans
Indexer: Trish Wittenstein
Print Buyer: Anna Chin

Contents

To Jordan with love,
for whom all good things
will be possible.

Preface

As an African American and a black family scholar, my long-standing interest in black families is both personal and professional. On a personal level, I have recognized the importance and cultural uniqueness of the African American family. On a professional level, my interest in black life and culture was academically nurtured during my undergraduate years at Clark University. My interests eventually focused on black families and I began a systematic exploration of African American or black families while a graduate student at the University of California at Berkeley. The family in slavery was the subject of my dissertation. From that point, I moved on to looking at more contemporary problems and issues of family.

Motivation for the Study

A review of the literature on families reveals that published research on black families has been sparse; and, until recently, there has been almost no attention paid to black middle-class families. With the exception of Frazier's (1957) *Black Bourgeoisie,* research efforts concerned with black families have focused on non-middle-class black families. In the past several years, a limited number of scholars have begun to examine the particulars of this neglected-by-research family group (see Barnes, 1985; McAdoo, 1978, 1988; Willie, 1991a, 1991b). There remains much to be said, and many of the nuances of this type of black family are yet to be explored.

Except for the late 1960s through the 1970s, when we saw a prolif-eration of works published about blacks and black families, much of the research on black families has been conceptualized in the pejorative. Much of what has been written about black families has focused on the problems in black life and black families, including those of teen preg-nancy and, in recent years, the plight of the black underclass. Thus, the view of the black family conveyed by the contemporary literature on blacks is heavily weighted in the direction of the problematic, if not the pathological.

Struck by the paucity in the literature of models of strong black fami-lies, strong middle-class black families, and the preponderance of focus on pejorative issues, I grew enthusiastic about filling this void. It seemed logical to me that if solutions were to be sought for the myriad of prob-lems that plague so many contemporary black families, one must begin by looking at strong black families—those who had survived and achieved against the odds. If we could identify those factors that func-tioned to bolster and sustain successful black families, perhaps from here we could make proscriptions for those black families that needed strengthening.

Although the concerns of non-middle-class black families are impor-tant and the problems that exist among black families due to poverty and other social factors are urgent and crucial, we need to know more about more stable and positive models of black families as well. This is not to say that positive models of family do not exist among the poor and working class, for they do. Rather, that we are more likely to find them among middle-class families because of the economic stability that they enjoy; the opposite of which is causal of the array of problems affecting those families for whom this is lacking. Research agendas should continue to focus attention on families in our society that suffer disadvantage, but should also focus increased attention on the array of families that constitute the whole of black families. Furthermore, models of stable black families are needed to find solutions for families that need assistance. We learn about strengths and how to be successful from strong, successful families.

In narrowing my focus to a specific population for study, I considered looking at families by occupational grouping including the clergy and physicians. But, it seemed potentially most valuable to focus on black corporate families because they are the newest among occupational groups of successful black families. The corporation, whose doors were closed to African Americans in professional and managerial capacities for so many decades, appears to be the new avenue for achievement of middle-class status for blacks.

THE PREVIOUS RESEARCH EFFORTS
FROM WHICH THIS WORK FLOWS

Although there are many black family scholars on whose shoulders I stand in developing this work (Walter Allen, Joyce Ladner, Harriette McAdoo, Marie Peters, Robert Staples, Charles Willie, and others), there is another handful of scholars, some living, some no longer with us, whom I am compelled to name. Their writings uniquely informed and inspired this work. My first inspiration was W. E. B. DuBois (1908), the father of black family studies, who authored the first major empirical work in U.S. sociology in 1899, and to whom eternal praise is due. I was also inspired by E. Franklin Frazier, a student of DuBois's and one of the most (if not the most) prominent African American sociologists of the 20th century. Frazier (1939, 1957) helped focus research on the Negro family in the United States and the Negro middle class. But he left us wanting a fuller view of black families, one that also shed light on its more positive attributes and on the nature of that experience. Andrew Billingsley (1968), in *Black Families in White America,* gave us a new look at black families and a more positive view of middle-class black families. But his structuralist approach offered only one angle or perspective. Robert Hill (1971) focused attention on the historical strengths of black families, which traditionally helped these families to survive. He wrote on the heels of what, to that point in time with little exception, had been a highly pejorative literature. He wrote about black families across different socioeconomic classes and statuses. An important aspect of his contribution to black family study and family strengths literature was his isolation of the strengths of African American families from family strengths in general. Bart Landry (1987), in *The New Black Middle Class,* presented a more up-to-date report on the experiences of the contemporary African American middle class, providing insight several decades beyond the view that Frazier offered on the experiences of African Americans by race and by class. Finally, in this decade, Feagin and Sikes (1994) highlight the insidious persistence of racism for blacks in the middle class.

It is my hope that this book will be of value to a broad-ranged audience. Specifically, it should be a useful tool for practitioners for proscribing family health and strength. It should be useful for scholars in increasing their understanding of black middle-class family dynamics, particularly black corporate families. Ideally, it will assist those in corporate employ, particularly those in management, in enhancing strategies for enriching corporate life and increasing productivity. Finally, it should assist blacks and other minorities as well in their climb up the corporate ladder.

Please note that the names of the respondents in this study have been changed and the names of the corporations in which they are employed withheld to maintain confidentiality.

Acknowledgments

There are many to whom I wish to express a most sincere thank-you for their encouragement, support, and assistance in completing this project: to Jim Nageotte, Margaret Zusky, and the staff of Sage Publications for their interest in and enthusiasm for the book; to those who assisted with providing the sample for the study; to the corporate managers and their families who participated in this research by providing the data for it, for their candor, enthusiasm, and accommodation; to my departmental colleagues for their professional and personal encouragement; to Mary Bruno and the staff of the Iona College Information Technology Resource Center for numerous hours of technical support; and to Leona Uju Ogbogu, Dora Mendez, John Pahucki, and Peter Byrons for their assistance with library work and miscellanea.

Much appreciation and sincere thanks go to Bert Adams and David Klein, who I have admired and whose work I have respected for many years, for their direction and the careful reading of this book. They were demanding, yet wonderful to work with. Thanks also to my father, Earl Van Dyke Toliver, for numerous hours of loving child care and for reading earlier versions of the book. Unbounded thanks and affection go to my husband, Stephen J. Perry, for his unconditional support, praise, and encouragement in my work and for this project from start to finish, and to my son, Jordan Toliver Perry, for being such a special joy. To all of my friends, relatives, and colleagues who spurred me on to complete *Black Families in Corporate America*—many thanks.

PART I

The Study

1

Background and Statement
of the Problem

Lerone Bennett, in the *Eyes on the Prize* (Carson, Garrow, Harding, & Hine, 1989) audio program series, borrowing from turn of the century social thinker Vilfredo Pareto, used the powerful statement, "Much has changed, yet, only to remain the same," as the major theme in his discussion on black progress in the United States. This phrase, in many ways, speaks to the tone of this book. Although the book amplifies the first truth of this statement, highlighting the remarkable achievements of upwardly mobile black men and women in America's corporations, and of the achievements of their families, the latter truth, although perhaps spoken in a softer voice, also resounds. In the past two to three decades, we have watched blacks open new doors and entrench themselves in new social, political, and economic arenas; we have also seen that many of the same problems, or new versions of the same problems, persist. This chapter is offered as background to this study.

The New Race Relations: The Confusion
and Illusion of Black Progress

If we could turn the clock back 35 years or so and juxtapose the United States then with the United States now, one could readily observe the night-and-day difference in the legal status of African Americans. The victories of the civil rights movement included changes and new opportunities for blacks in things as diverse as how they could use public transportation and public buildings, to the type of employment open to them. Coupled with full equality under the law, the movement had integration as its goal. The achievement of integration, blacks thought, would bring about equal opportunity in areas such as housing, education, employment, and particularly in the political process. With integration, they also hoped to gain from their fellow Americans respect as citizens with full constitutional rights, and as human beings. In short, integration held the promise of a better life for future generations of African Americans.

As with any social movement, the full effects of change are difficult to anticipate. Also, change is usually less than complete or perfect. So, too, it has been with the civil rights movement; blacks could not have foreseen exactly the fruits that their struggles would reap. They thought that the achievement of the goals of the movement would solve their problems. They did not foresee that the goals and gains of the civil rights movement would result in a whole new set of unanticipated consequences and problems.

Specifically, there are three conditions or factors that have caused black progress to be less than perfect.

1. *Black progress has not been evenly distributed within the black community across class lines. The gains made by the middle class account for the bulk of the progress. Nor has progress positioned blacks equal to whites in areas such as income.* The national trend in the past few decades has been that the income gap between the lower and upper two fifths of the population has widened as the rich get richer and the poor get poorer. Because black families are concentrated in the lower two fifths of U.S. families, generally they have gained comparatively little. Among employed blacks, black families earn only 55% of what white families earn. Although more black families have attained middle-class status than ever before, their number still equals only one third of all black families. Furthermore, the American dream seems unattainable for many of the children born into the middle class who are not doing as well as or better than their parents. The upper middle class is the only group among blacks that has increased its wealth. The proportion of families in this group, however, has gotten smaller. Dual-headed families, in which both partners are educated, do well, earning 80% of what similar white families earn.

2. *Progress, in the form of integration, has been achieved only in some sectors of some arenas.* For example, with respect to housing, some neighborhoods, sections of cities, and whole communities still remain restricted to whites via selective real estate sales practices, hostile treatment of blacks on the part of white residents, and unspoken policies that blacks are not welcome. "White flight" from neighborhoods as blacks move in is not uncommon. Restrictive covenants still exist in some locales and are informally upheld. The bulk of the black population continues to reside in predominantly black neighborhoods. With respect to jobs, education, and income, blacks again are not fully integrated into the mainstream, being restricted with few exceptions within occupational groups to the lowest-level jobs, with the majority of black physicians still being trained at the small handful of black medical colleges, and with the bulk of black incomes falling short of the national median.

3. *The conservative political climate of the Reagan and Bush years and the emergence of the New Right has relaxed, abandoned, and all but obliterated support for government policy that was so critical to stabilizing and ensuring the continuance of black progress.* This has thwarted black progress on two levels. First, it has impeded (even decreased) upward mobility (especially among, but not limited to, the poor and working class) by curtailing affirmative action programs, and education and job training programs. The work of Hershberg, Burstein, Ericksen, Greenberg, and Yancey (1979), and others argues for the importance of affirmative action policy initiatives and enforcement by the government if the problem of black underachievement is to be solved. The effect of enacting such policies would have implications across class lines. Second, it has sanctioned and encouraged antiblack sentiment within the mainstream, among whites, by promoting the false notion that there no longer is a race problem and that those blacks who have made it have worked hard, and those who have not are lazy, criminal, less gifted, or suffer from deficient values. Successful blacks and their achievements are used as evidence that there is no race problem.

An important fact when talking of achieving the goals of the civil rights movement is that we have only partially achieved these goals. Although equal education is now the law, in many cases it is still not the reality. Although there is equal opportunity employment under the law and affirmative action (now waning) in hiring, institutional racism and gatekeeping continue to serve as obstacles to the employment and promotion of blacks in business and industry. In short, the position of blacks in the United States today is still less than equal.

EFFECTS OF DESEGREGATION:
THE DOWNSIDE OF PROGRESS

The gains made by the civil rights movement were not a panacea to all African Americans for all of their problems; however, the benefits to some, although not all, were great. Those black men, women, and children whose experiences are the focus of this book are among the small group for whom the struggles of the 1950s and 1960s have paid off. Because of desegregation, achievement in new economic and social arenas has been made possible. Among blacks, they are part of an elite whose lives may be characterized by others as being made up of all the "right stuff."

These men and women enjoy high-status positions as managers in corporate America. They are highly educated, and their children have achieved or are on the road to achieving the same. Among the older children of this group, we find many who are graduates of or enrolled in Ivy League schools and other of the finest institutions of higher education in the country. The younger children are enrolled in preparatory and other private schools, and public schools that rank high in teacher involvement, facilities and materials, and academic excellence. The neighborhoods in which they reside tend to be more affluent than average. The cars they drive are likely to be new and sometimes expensive. They vacation in ordinary, close to home as well as far off, exotic places. Their homes, cars, and other possessions are indicative of a lifestyle that in modest terms could be described as comfortable. Although there is a sizable range in status and affluence within this group depending on income and length of tenure in corporate employ, all of the managers in this study have managed to slice off for themselves and for their families a healthy piece of the American pie.

Their accomplishments symbolize and are suggestive of many things. For some Americans, the success of this group of elites would seem to provide proof that equal opportunity for all races in our society has been achieved. For others in the black community, it suggests that the American dream is attainable for blacks, even if only for a few—whose experiences perhaps are cases of exception to the rule. Others still may be envious, or resentful of what this group has achieved in "making it" in corporate America.

Theoretically and realistically, it is the case with any social movement that change is always less than perfect. Although this is true of the civil rights movement in the sense that progress was not experienced evenly or amply throughout the black community, it is true in another sense as well. We can also say that the movement did not reap perfect progress in that the benefits gained by the black middle and upper middle classes have not come without costs.

Two important realities affecting the central themes and many of the major topical concerns of this book should be identified at this point. These realities are at the heart of the effects of desegregation. First, desegregation in jobs, housing, education, and on social levels, to the extent to which desegregation has occurred, has thrust blacks and whites together in ways that they have never been before. And, second, desegregation has enabled more affluent or middle-class blacks to move beyond the confines of the inner cities, which often means beyond the bounds of the black community, to acquire better-quality housing, education for their children, and a generally enhanced quality of life. These two facts, but especially the latter, have dramatically affected all walks of black life. Together, these realities have created new problems for the black middle class and for black Americans, in general.

Specifically,

- "Baby Bumps" (children of Black Upwardly Mobile Professionals) are now at risk for having their black identities "whitewashed" because they are less rooted in the black experience and lack contact with others who are black. They are much less likely to experience black social life and culture (outside of the family context) that comes close to that experienced by the same class peers of previous generations.[1]
- Middle-class blacks can move into jobs where their peers are white (blacks and whites in the middle class now work side by side), where they may perceive a lack of control over their work environment, and where they are certainly likely to experience feelings of isolation from other blacks in their work lives.
- There is a schism within the black community because affluent blacks can now move away and lose day-to-day touch with the realities of the black community. The result has been that the daily vicissitudes of life for the

two groups have grown qualitatively different and dramatically more divergent.

There was a time in the very recent past when all or most of the social interactions experienced by black middle-class Americans were with other blacks, and included other blacks from all walks of life. They lived in a black community. Whether they were janitors or doctors, they were likely to have contact with each other. Although separations existed even then among the classes, how could they lose sight of their blackness? This same janitor and doctor saw each other at church, their children often went to the same schools, they were treated by the same physicians, and in many other ways their life experiences were connected or interfaced.

Blacks in the middle class who were doctors, lawyers, or ministers not only had a black constituency or clientele but tended to be autonomous in the context of work. For example, those who were middle class and employed in occupations such as those mentioned here were often their own bosses. Today, black middle-class managers do not have such autonomy on the job and work in companies that are white controlled.

If we frame this discussion in the context of the most recent economic realities, we will find another factor contributing to the divergence among black lifestyles. In the past approximately two decades, the gap between the "haves" and the "have nots" in this society has widened. The economic realities, and in turn the lifestyles, of the most and least affluent in this country have grown more divergent. This is true within both white and black America. Specifically, the most affluent among blacks have increased their wealth, whereas poor blacks in this country have become more impoverished and have increased in number.

The change from the solid and comparatively unitary nature of the black community before, and the fragmentation and increased social distance now of the various sectors of the black community after desegregation, have resulted in deleterious effects on blacks as a whole. For the janitor's child, or other poor or working-class children, these effects manifest themselves as a lack of role models of upward mobility and an inability to provide examples of alternative choices of lifestyles and behaviors within a black context, which would make these choices appear more relevant to and attainable in their own lives.[2] It also means the lack of a peer group whose parents can realistically provide for their children the opportunity to achieve academic excellence and thereby the means to achieve success in their lives. For the middle-class child, it means a lack of a regular, pervasive experience of black culture in one's day-to-day life, and a distancing from one's black social and cultural heritage, resulting in an absence of significant opportunities for the development of a black sense of self. For adults of all sectors of black society, the result is a lack of support, understanding, compassion, connection, inspiration, reinforcement, and hope for today and for the future.

THE CONTINUING SIGNIFICANCE OF RACE

Wilson (1978a, 1978b) argued in *The Declining Significance of Race,* "the growing importance of class and the decreasing significance of race in determining blacks' chances in life." Willie (1978) argued in *The Inclining Significance of Race,* his response to Wilson's analysis, for the inclining significance of race "especially for middle-class blacks who, because of school desegregation and affirmative action and other integration programs, are coming into direct contact with whites." In the minds of many scholars and intellectuals, the class-over-race debate appears to be one that is settled, and settled in fairly absolute terms. For a significant group of scholars in the field of race relations and within the discipline of sociology in general, as well as other disciplines, class, not race, is the determining factor for progress and successful mobility in contemporary U.S. society. For these scholars, virtually the only causal stratification variable of black achievement that is recognized is class.

Despite the well-structured, fact-based arguments of Willie and others who provide evidence that race persists as a powerful deterrent to black success across all class lines, this reality has not been grasped or admitted to by all. Wilson, the leading proponent of the class-over-race argument, has provided a basis for substantiating the claims of those who are no longer willing to admit to the pervasiveness of racism as a sickness that plagues our society.

Why the tendency for some to admit to class and not race? For some, it may be ignorance of the realities of the minority experience in the United States. For others, the class-over-race argument may be more palatable. Some may perceive class bias as a more palatable form of inequality—less insidious than race bias. Admitting the existence of a classist versus racist society may in some ways be less offensive to those who view themselves as progressive-minded Americans.

Although class certainly is a determinant of the opportunities afforded all Americans—black, white, and other—we cannot attribute the primary cause of limited black progress to class alone. (And, in fact, Wilson, especially in his 1978c work, does not do this). Particularly in the case of middle- and upper-middle-class blacks, the argument of class as the only prime causal variable in determining progress would not hold. By way of example, the experiences of black managers in the corporate world today would certainly not support the class-over-race argument. For them, the significance of race undeniably continues.

Although the initial formulations of these arguments were published nearly two decades ago, the arguments of both Wilson and Willie certainly had validity then and continue to do so now. Neither should or can be dismissed. Furthermore, the arguments and factors used to support them are neither entirely parallel nor entirely contradictory. But, the continuing importance of race as a key factor in determining the experiences of blacks who have achieved relatively high status in contemporary society remains particularly salient and should not be understated.

In the case of those successful, upwardly mobile blacks, including black corporate managers and their families, who have achieved middle-class status, the factor of class no longer functions as an impediment to continued success or quality of life. Looking at the obstacles or factors that diminish life chances, the thesis of class over race does not wholly apply. Even when the lower- to middle-class boundary is crossed, the factor of race is, and indeed remains, highly salient. In this book, the variable of race and its effects on the lives of this select type of middle-class family (black corporate) will be explored.

It is in large part precisely because of the continuing significance of race that explanatory models of stress, the family, and even gender politics that are based on the white nuclear family and the male white corporate manager do not apply in the case of black corporate managers and their families. The persistence of racism in our society creates very different realities for blacks and whites. It affects the work lives of African Americans, their mate selection opportunities, their parenting behaviors, their roles as husbands and wives, and a variety of other areas of social living. Indeed, race is a powerful factor affecting the overall life satisfaction and experiences of African Americans today.

IT "AIN'T NO CRYSTAL STAIR",
IT'S THE CEILING THAT'S MADE OF GLASS

Although several blacks have made it to significant, high-level positions of power in corporate America, the upward climb for blacks in corporate management is often halted well before reaching the highest levels. After a hard struggle just to enter the corporate ranks, blacks with an eye toward upward mobility soon find their way blocked by what has been called the "glass ceiling." Such a ceiling allows a view of the top levels of management, while at the same time it serves as a barrier that keeps those levels just out of reach. Although there has been a significant increase in the number of blacks in the corporate world over the past 25 years, and a few who have made it to key positions, closer examination of the distribution of blacks within the U.S.'s corporate hierarchy reveals a less than perfect picture (see "In Good Company," 1988).

Analysis of where blacks are located in corporate America shows that the bulk of blacks are in nonmanagerial and first-line managerial positions. Blacks can finally get their feet through the door; the difficulty now lies in making it up the stairs. In recent years, there has been an increase in the numbers of managers, but few have ascended to the highest ranks, and there are proportionately fewer than the number of whites. According to the findings of research conducted by Korn/Ferry International (Johnson, 1987, p. 20), there were only four black senior executive officers immediately below the chief executive level among Fortune 100 companies. In 1992, only 0.4% of the senior-level decision-making managers in Fortune 1000 industrial and Fortune 500 service companies were black—97% were white males according to U.S. Labor Secretary Robert Reich's "Glass Ceiling Commission Report" (McCoy, 1995). Mainstreaming blacks and other minorities into corporate America is not just a matter of getting the right numbers of blacks into the corporate world. It also means allowing their unrestricted access to the highest ranks of that world.

The state of corporate America as we move through the 1990s can still be described as being racially and ethnically stratified. The helms of power are still elusive for blacks who come to the corporate workplace talented and well prepared, well educated, and experienced. Full integration of blacks into all levels of corporate management remains a distant cry from reality. This situation is unfortunate for the U.S. corporate business sector, which is underusing a valuable human resource pool at the same time that the business sector is rapidly losing ground as the world leader in industry. It is unfortunate, too, for the black corporate manager (and his or her family) who is able to compete, perform, and excel and is deserving of the opportunity to achieve.

The Problem at Hand

The subjects of this book are ordinary people. Yet, they are extra-ordinary people. They are your next-door neighbors in urban centers and adjacent suburban areas. They work hard for a living, are God-fearing individuals, and love their children. On the other hand, they are an exceptional cadre that has experienced high levels of achievement against tremendous odds and in the face of incredible obstacles. Their superior talent, intellect, drive, and luck have made them unique among their social group/category. They are black corporate managers, and their families.

Broadly, the book will look at black managers and their families, and their sources of stress and strength. The overriding question that is addressed in this research is, "How has their participation in corporate America affected the lives of black corporate managers and their families, and, to perhaps a lesser extent, how does the factor of race affect the lives of black corporate families and their members?" Two underlying aims of the book are to raise the issue of how black corporate managers and their families can enjoy the benefits of their success without losing their African American cultural identity, and, to suggest that corporations consider the benefits of creating a totally integrated multicultural workforce for the well-being of its African American families—an initiative that, in turn, will benefit the corporation (see Jaynes & Williams, 1989 for a full description of total institutional integration).

The specific questions that the book seeks to address include the following:

- How is the profile of corporate family stress composed uniquely for black families?
- What are the strengths of black corporate families? In response to this question, the guiding hypothesis is that the five strengths of black families identified by Robert Hill (1971) (strong kinship bonds, strong work

orientation, adaptability of family roles, strong achievement orientation, strong religious orientation) will prevail within black corporate families.

- What are the interactive effects of corporate employment and inter-personal relationships including family and mate selection for black women managers?

- What factors make the relocation experience different for black manage-rial families? In this connection, I hypothesize that the presence of a black community as a *gemeinschaft* functions to ease the experience of reloca-tion.

- How are the wives of black managers affected by their husbands' employ in corporate America?

- What are the special issues of black middle-class parents in child rearing.

- How does race marginality in the corporation affect black managers and their families?

FOCUS, ASSUMPTIONS,
AND DELIMITATIONS

This book is about family—both for those who have it and those who want it. It is about whole families and the individual members who constitute its parts. It looks at the multiple breakdown of family rela-tions—the husband-wife dyad, parents and children, nuclear and ex-tended, and mate selection. It is concerned with individuals as members of families and their concerns about family issues. Although each chapter title reflects its specific focus, the theme of family and the importance of it underlie each chapter.

The book explores the subject of race for black families. This research is predicated on the assumption that race makes a difference. That is, I have assumed that race is a salient factor affecting the lives of black corporate managers and their families. I do not wish to "solve" the race versus class debate, and it is beyond the scope of this study to determine whether race versus class is the more powerful determinant of or has a greater impact on life experiences for black corporate managers. I do wish to see how race is a factor that determines and influences their experiences—how does race make a difference?

The sources of data for the research were 191 managers, 102 spouses, and 33 children of corporate managers. All managers were drawn from Fortune 100 companies headquartered in the northeastern part of the United States. Data were collected from 1991 through December 1994.

SOME TERMS TO BE CLARIFIED

The term *corporate family* is used to describe those families in which one or both heads of household, in the case of this study husband and/or wife, are employed in corporate America. Similarly, the term *corporate managerial family* is used to describe families with one or both heads of household employed in management positions in corporations. They are viewed as corporate "families" because this research both assumes and attempts to explore the ways in which corporate employment of one member affects families collectively as well as the dyadic relationships individually. Furthermore, these families have some distinctive features or characteristics. These features include that they are typically highly mobile, enjoy a higher level of affluence relative to the median income and lifestyle of the general population (especially in the case of managers in this study because they are employed in Fortune 100 companies and are therefore likely to have higher annual salaries on average than managers employed in comparable positions in smaller corporations), and sometimes, but not always, live in communities populated by a sizable percentage of families who also have a member employed in corporate America (see Margolis, 1979). To assist newly hired or newly relocated families, corporations, through their employee assistance programs, often refer these families to certain schools, places to shop, and other locales to frequent. One can assume that these characteristics are likely to effect some commonality of culture of experience.

On the subject of *social class,* the families included in this study would be classified on the basis of income and education as middle class and, more specifically, as upper middle class. But, the term *elite* might also be used to describe them. This may suggest a contradiction in the use of terms but, in fact, in the case of black or African Americans, it is not. This point warrants further explanation. Class operationalizes, divides, and is defined somewhat differently for blacks. That is, to be black and upper middle class is to be elite within the black community and within U.S. society (Billingsley, 1968). Specifically, although there is a growing number of black millionaires, if we use this level of economic net worth as a benchmark of elite status, they are still relatively few in number vis-à-vis the percentage of the same in the total population. Their number can be considered to be negligible. We might consider individuals to be elite within their own community if they rank within the top percentiles of income for that community. We might also consider individuals to be elite if they distinguish themselves as the highest economic achievers of their group (race) within the larger population. On the basis of these two criteria of accomplishment, the subjects of this research can be considered elite, not inconsistent with upper middle class. Although there is variation within this group, the group of black corporate managers enjoys the best, high-status lifestyle particulars to be enjoyed by any and all blacks in this country. The top level of the income or total net asset bracket among all blacks is much lower, and this uppermost strata of black economic worth is much less heavily populated than that of whites. Although there is variation in the income and the lifestyles that it affords within this group, black corporate managers economically and educationally equal the cream of the crop within the black community, and the best and the brightest of Americans who are black.

THE CHAPTER-BY-CHAPTER PLAN

Specifically, Chapter 1, by way of background for this study, has attempted to identify some of the forces and factors that have affected both the presence and status of blacks in the United States—including blacks in the corporate world and in their communities, and to begin to define (and delimit) the nature and scope of this study.

The first part of Chapter 2 focuses on the general concept of stress, reviews some of the literature on stress theory, and applies the concept of stress to corporate workers and their families. In the second part of the chapter, I explore the question, "What is a strong, healthy family?" Family strengths previously identified by social scientists are considered with particular focus on the traditionally touted black family strengths.

Chapter 3 elaborates on the methodology employed. It discusses the data needed, the tools and techniques for gathering data, the nature of the questions asked, the description of the corporations represented in the sample, the analysis, and the weaknesses and reliability of the study.

The next part of the book attempts to address the study's substantive concerns. Chapter 4 focuses on sources of stress for and strengths of black corporate managers and their families. The added potential stress for black managers and their families caused by being the target of individual race prejudice and the victims of institutional racism is discussed and, hence, an alternative conceptualization of corporate stress for black managers is offered. In the second part of this chapter, the issue of whether or not the black family strengths identified in the literature exist is explored, in particular those identified by Robert Hill (1971), with specific reference to corporate managerial families.

Chapter 5 discusses black women and their historical experience with work, with special emphasis on contemporary problems of racism and sexism for black female corporate managers. The chapter will also explore the interpersonal relationships of successful black women with men, their families, and their community.

The next three chapters focus on the multiple varieties of demands the corporation places on the family. New perspectives and respondents' views on relocation are offered in Chapter 6. The notion of wives incorporation in men's work and its changing nature is explored in Chapter 7, devoting attention to the ways in which wives' activities support the work and familial roles of their husbands, and the degree of mutual inclusiveness of home and work. Special black child-rearing concerns, in particular, parental fears in reference to the "race neutralizing" of black middle-class youth affected by the corporate lifestyle are examined in Chapter 8.

Chapter 9 presents and critiques the traditional conception of marginality focusing on a more positive formulation of the concept. The experiences and life situations of black corporate families are used to illustrate elements of this more positive view. Chapter theme: There are positive as well as negative aspects of being different.

Returning to the central concerns of this research relating to black managers and their families, Chapter 10 summarizes and concludes the main ideas of the book and provides further discussion and suggestions for future research. The interactive effects of the corporate culture, family, and productivity are explored in this final chapter. The chapter attempts to illustrate the ways in which the presence of blacks and other minorities, including women, have transformed corporate enterprise into a new reality. Successful management of diversity and its possibilities for increased productivity will be pointed to. Following from these notions, it is suggested that traditional notions of corporate culture need to be expanded to reflect the heterogeneity of the contemporary corporate population, and the argument is made for further exploration of the impact of racism as well as the impact of the family sphere on corporate productivity. Last, the realm of corporate responsibility is expanded to include greater consideration of the importance of the families of corporate managers.

Notes

1. The exception to this statement is, of course, their experiences inside the family context, but we know that the family is not the only socializing agent affecting the child's developmental outcome. Other agents including schools, peers, and the media are at play and function in ways that reinforce one another in creating for the child a view of the world that is anglocentric in its cultural orientation.

2. Although some might take issue with the assertion that solidarity existed in the black community prior to desegregation, there was certainly a greater interfacing and a crossing of paths among those of different economic and educational strata. Whereas blacks from different walks of life may not have broken bread together, they were more likely to have attended the same church, used the services of the same black physician, and, in the South, to have shared the same balcony at the segregated movie theater than would be the case today. Although poor black youngsters of today might have a greater number of distant role models to emulate, in years past, they likely had a greater access to more proximate role models.

2

Corporate Family Stress, Black Family Strengths

The Literature

This research focuses on the sources of stress and strengths of black families in corporate America. Some of the specific questions related to stress and strengths that guide this investigation include the following: Why do black corporate managers and their families experience stress? How can such stress be handled? Do black families possess the resources necessary for dealing effectively with stress? To answer these questions, it will be helpful to review what scholars and researchers have discovered to date about stress and the strengths required to handle it. Therefore, this chapter will explore some of the literature on stress and family strengths. Let us begin with theories on stress, to be followed by a treatment of family strengths, including especially black family strengths.

What Research Has Taught Us About Stress

Although stress in both its positive and negative forms ("eustress" and "distress") has been a subject of study for more than half a century, the focus of concern has varied according to the perspective of the researcher: Biomedical researchers such as Selye (1956, 1974, 1983) examined physiological reactions to stress; psychologists like Lazarus (1966) and Kutash (Kutash & Schlesinger, 1980) were more interested in what individuals and groups perceived to be stressful situations;

anthropologists compared cultural definitions of and reactions to stress; sociologists looked at class, race, sex, age, and occupation as factors shaping the stressful experience.

In the mid-1960s, a number of researchers began to explore the family's reaction to stress. Reuben Hill's (1965) ABCX model, which has its roots earlier in the literature (Reuben Hill, 1949), represents one attempt to provide a conceptual framework within which to understand how families define and respond to stressful situations. In Hill's model, A (the stressful event) interacts with B (the family's resources for coping with such events) and C (the family's definition of the event). The nature of this interaction produces X (the crisis; p. 32).

In their study of families in crisis, Parad and Caplan (1965) elaborated on what Reuben Hill had described as a family's "crisis meeting resources," that is, the B component of the ABCX model. They took into account *"family lifestyle . . .* value systems, communication networks, and role systems; *intermediate problem-solving mechanisms . . .* the family lifestyle in action; and the *need-response pattern . . .* the ways . . . the family . . . perceives, respects, and satisfies the basic needs of its individual members" (p. 57, emphasis in the original).

McCubbin and Patterson (1981, 1982, 1983) further revised Reuben Hill's ABCX model, developing what they called the double ABCX model, which takes into account the ripple effect caused by the initial stressor and the response to it, and accommodates the possibility of multiple stressors impinging on a family. Assessing the nature of these stresses and the resources and modes a family has for dealing with them, they described the family's response to a crisis as being either "bonadaptive" or "maladaptive."

These three studies of families under stress share an important feature: They all regard stress as an interactive rather than a static phenomenon—a process rather than an event. Although researchers have taught us much about the complex nature of stress, the theories they have generated tend to be limited in that they apply to a specific setting, institution, or social group, thus failing to take into account that the lives of individuals span a number of different settings and roles and that experiences in one setting necessarily influence those in another. Until recently, few studies, for example, have considered the mutual impact of stress at home and in the workplace. As a result, corporations often fail to acknowledge the connections, both positive and negative, between the domains of family and work.

Piotrkowski, Rapoport, and Rapoport (1987), in their review of research on families and work, noted that whereas social scientists have traditionally linked the social institutions of the family and the economy, paradoxically, family and work continued to be treated as separate spheres. Only recently have scholars in a variety of disciplines begun to link the treatment of family life issues to the particular subfields of their disciplines related to work (e.g., in sociology—family to work and occupations, in psychology—family to industrial psychology). Those who have made the family-work connection and have focused on the impact of either one on the other or reciprocally include Ammons, Nelson, and Wodarski (1982); Apter (1994); Archer (1969); Bernstein (1985); Blau and Ehrenberg (1997); Boss, McCubbin, and Lester (1979); Broman (1991); Dinnerstein (1992); Elman and Gilbert (1984); Epstein (1971); Gaylord (1984); Gerstel and Gross (1984); Gilbert, Holahan, and Manning (1981); Greiff and Munter (1980); Hanks and Sussman (1990); Harrison and Minor (1978); Kluwer, Heesink, and van de Vliert (1996); Kozmetsky and Kozmetsky (1981); Malmaud (1984); McCubbin, Boss, Wilson, and Lester (1980); Menaghan and Parcel (1990); Michaels (1992); Moen (1983); Piotrkowski and Repetti (1984); Pleck (1977); Riggs (1990); Simpson and England (1981); Staines and Pleck (1983); Toliver (1986); Volling and Belsky (1991); Voydanoff (1984); Voydanoff and Kelly (1984); Winett and Neale (1981); and Zvonkovic, Greaves, Schmiege, and Hall (1996). Those who look at work-family stress include Crouter (1984); Eckenrode and Gore (1990); Elman and Gilbert (1984); Epstein (1971); Gilbert et al. (1981); Skinner (1983); and Voydanoff and Kelly (1984). Focusing specifically on corporate families and stress are Ammons et al. (1982); Fishman and Cherniss (1990); Friedman (1987); Kofodimos (1993); Voydanoff (1980); and Zedeck (1992).

Of the 43 life events used by Holmes and Rahe (1967) to measure stress, approximately one third had to do with marriage and family. Similarly, Gherman (1981) found that "stressors connected with marriage are the most common causes of depression," a condition that would surely affect the manager's ability to function optimally in the workplace. But just as stress at home can influence effectiveness at work, so can stress at work affect the quality of life at home, either by creating new problems or exacerbating old ones.

WHY CORPORATE MANAGERS AND
THEIR FAMILIES EXPERIENCE STRESS

To identify the sources of stress experienced by black corporate managers and their families, it is important to distinguish between what this study calls workplace stress and family work-related stress. Workplace stress can be attributed to a manager's anxiety about performance, competitiveness among workers, politics in the office, narrowness of role definitions, long hours of work, or the demands of travel. This kind of stress affects the manager directly. In contrast, family work-related stress affects both the manager and his or her family. It can be caused by the upheaval resulting from geographic relocation, the competing demands of work and family roles—especially for female managers, the absence of the corporate manager from the home because of long work hours or business travel, or the dependence of the corporate wife in some instances on her husband for identity and status (see Piotrkowski et al., 1987 for a review of the full array of family work-related problems and stressors identified in the literature on work and family).

For example, the "problem" of the corporate wife has been the focus of a number of studies (Archer, 1969; Seidenberg, 1973; Upson, 1974; Wyse, 1970). Archer pointed out that although a manager's wife can assist her husband in building and maintaining his career, she can also be a source of worry for him because he often feels responsible for her contentment and self-esteem. Because the nature of their involvement with the corporation differs, what may be regarded by the husband as a positive step may be experienced by his wife as somewhat negative.

Relocation is another example of a potentially stressful experience to which corporate families are often subject. Also, it can have quite different meanings for a husband whose job necessitates a relocation and his wife. Because work is the primary source of status for males in this society, a husband's status is generally bolstered by a promotion to a job in a new location. The sources of a wife's sense of status and self-esteem are generally more diverse and diffused: They may derive from a job or career, involvement in the PTA or in local politics, membership in a social or community organization, or simply from having found the right butcher or hairdresser in her community. In any of these cases, relocation will disrupt the wife's life, cutting her off from her source of status and diminishing her self-esteem and sense of mastery. At best, she will have to accommodate herself to the demands of a new environment. Because a wife's credentials are less likely than those of her husband to be transferable, whether she works inside or outside the home, it is unlikely, even today, that relocation will result in an immediate increase in her status (see Chapters 7 and 6, this volume, respectively, for a more in-depth discussion of these topics).

SOURCES OF STRESS FOR BLACK MANAGERS
AND THEIR FAMILIES

There is only a limited body of research that focuses on black families and stress and black managers and stress. The research seems to suggest that workplace stress is the greater source of stress for black corporate managers. Furthermore, racism was identified as a major source of stress for these individuals and their families (see America, 1978; Davis, 1995; Davis & Watson, 1982; Dickens & Dickens, 1982; Fernandez, 1975, 1981; Irons & Moore, 1985; Jones, 1986; McAdoo, 1979; Nixon, 1985a, 1985b, 1985c; Staples & Johnson, 1993). Fernandez (1981) identified several ways in which blacks and other minorities in the corporate workplace are adversely affected by racism. For example, he found that blacks feel excluded from informal work groups and overlooked for promotions and important assignments because whites are often uncomfortable associating and working with them. Blacks and other minorities are also made to feel that they owe their jobs to hiring and staffing quotas rather than to their skills and competence. Lewis (1979), in his assessment of types of stress, identifies prejudice and racism as examples of "chronic stressors."

AN ALTERNATIVE CONCEPTUALIZATION OF STRESS
FOR BLACK CORPORATE MANAGERS

The beginning of this section of the chapter briefly explored some definitions and conceptual models of the stress phenomenon. We have also identified some of the typical sources of stress for corporate managers and further identified additional sources of stress unique to the experience of black managers and their families. If we use the double ABCX model (McCubbin & Patterson, 1983), which is more satisfying than competing models for the earlier stated reasons, as a framework for reviewing stress for corporate families, the makeup of the components of the model should differ sharply due especially to racism and cultural factors for black versus white managers and their families.

The elements contained in Components A (the stressor) and B (the family's crisis-meeting resources) will be different. Specifically, differences in family situation, coupled with racism and tokenism, build a different stress component (A) for black workers. Component B will be built differently, including such factors as wife's level of education relative to husband's and her avenues for self-actualization, but also especially reflecting the inclusion of traditional black family strengths and other support systems.

Juxtaposed to a model for white corporate families, a model for black corporate families would contain a stress Component A in which "family work-related stress" is outweighed by "workplace stress." A major factor in this reverse tipping of the scales whereby work problems overshadow family problems is the added key element of racism, which interacts with both types of stress. Also, because of racism, the nature of work and family problems is different. And, finally, the family's crisis-meeting resources, Component B, would include elements unique to the cultural traditions of black families. In Chapters 4 through 10, we will explore the presence of racism as a Component A element in the lives of black corporate managers and their families. We will also look at identifying sources of strength that include traditional black family strengths, which would be included in Component B. Thereby, we will be revising and further specifying the double ABCX Model (see Figure 2.1). In the next section, we will turn our attention to family strengths.

What Research Has Taught Us
About Black Family Strengths

Historically, the tone of the literature dealing with blacks and black families has, until the past two to three decades, been highly pejorative. Using a "clinical perspective," researchers have tended to focus on what makes certain families dysfunctional rather than on what makes others successful (Moynihan 1965; Myrdal, 1944). Fortunately, this tendency has now yielded to an increased concern for the identification of family strengths and a conceptualization of family health. Scholars like Allen

24

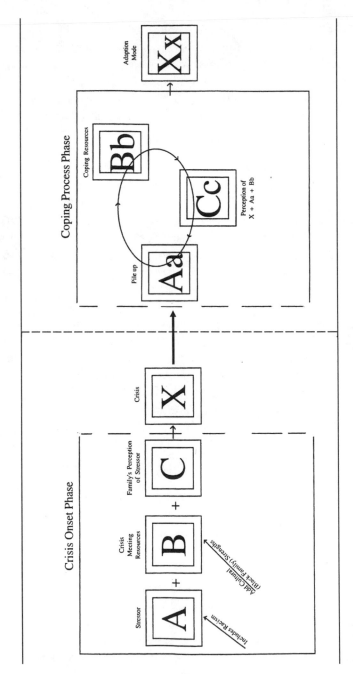

Figure 2.1. Alternative Conceptualization Double ABCX Model

(1978, 1986); Barnes (1985); Davis (1986); Davis (1995); Ellison (1990); Fine, Schewebel, and James-Myers (1987); Gershenfeld (1986); Goldscheider (1991); Greene (1995); Hill (1971); H. McAdoo (1988, 1993); J. L. McAdoo (1993); Pearson (1990); Peters (1978, 1981); Staples (1994); Taylor, Leashore, and Toliver (1988); Tolson (1990); and Willie (1988, 1991b) replaced the overridingly negative view with a richer and often more positive view of black family life and culture.

These extreme differences in attitude have yielded two distinct and contrasting images of the black family. It has been depicted as pathological, disorganized, and devoid of moral values on one hand and as strong and resilient on the other. Ladner (1971) pointed out that because much of the more positive literature was written in reaction to the negative tone of the earlier literature, the nature of the former has been constrained. The need to write reactively, understandable though it may be, has had the unfortunate effect of creating a defensive literature. In other words, both the overly negative and the reactively positive attitudes to research on black families have generated stereotypical images. The truth of the matter probably lies somewhere between the two. Black families are not all weak and unstable, but neither are they superfamilies. Taylor, Chatters, Tucker, and Lewis (1990), through their 1980s decade review of black family research, enable us to glean a more objective overview of the status of contemporary black families.

Noted historians and social science researchers have talked of the existence of certain cultural traits or black family strengths that have been key to the survival of blacks in the United States from the past to the present (see Blassingame, 1972; Genovese, 1972; Gutman, 1976; Hill, 1971). Some have argued that these traits are carryovers from African tradition (Nobles, 1974a, 1974b). Others have suggested that they are cultural adaptations that served as survival skills in the context of U.S. society (Gutman, 1976; Toliver, 1982). Whatever their origin, such strengths have been shown to exist and they are, to a large extent, unique to black families.

It is important to look for what makes families strong; however, it is also important to understand the problems and limitations associated with this endeavor. Embarking on a scholarly discourse on family strengths brings to the foreground many complex and divergent theoretical questions. For example:

— How should we approach the question of what makes a strong family?

— On what basis should one define a strong family?

— What can be considered a family strength?

— How many of these traits and in what combination must a family have to be considered healthy?

— Will the answers to these questions differ from culture to culture?

— Will they differ from family to family?

— Should families be considered strong or healthy only in relation to other families?

— Can any single theory of family strength capture and appreciate the complex nature of family interaction and family functioning?

Answers to these and other questions are many and complex.

To address some of these issues, we will do the following: We will review some of the existing literature on family strengths; we will suggest an alternative, interactive approach to the question, "What is a strong, healthy family?"

SELECTED LITERATURE ON FAMILY STRENGTHS

Otto (1962) was among the first of the family researchers to focus on the strengths of families. Included in his list of family strengths are the ability to provide for the physical, emotional, and spiritual needs of family members; the capacity to establish and maintain growth-producing relationships within and outside the family; and a concern for family unity, loyalty, and interfamilial cooperation. Many researchers since Otto have followed with similar delineations of family strengths and have also added new insights.

Robert Hill (1971) identified five traits that facilitated the survival, development, and stability of black families: strong kinship bonds, a strong work orientation, adaptability of family roles, a strong achievement orientation, and a strong religious orientation. Hill argued that the search to identify the existing strengths in black families was crucial to strengthening black families further: "If, as most scholars agree, there is a need to strengthen black families, then a first-order priority should be the identification of presently existing strengths, resources, and potentials" (p. 2).

Although Hill asserted that his list of strengths is not exclusive to black families, nor is it exhaustive of the total list of strengths that black families possess, he contended that the historical experience of racism has rendered the significance of these qualities unique among blacks: "The particular forms that these characteristics take among black families should be viewed as adaptations necessary for survival and advancement in a hostile environment" and should, therefore, be identified as "black family strengths" (Hill, 1971, p. 4).

As to the origin of Hill's strengths, my assessment is that they develop through the childhood socialization process. My sense is that their roots lie in the family of origin, including the extended family, although, in some cases, they may stem from other childhood sources, for example, through interaction with significant others and fictive kin (see Stack, 1996). These are the strengths brought to the corporation—or at least the seeds of them, by the black manager. How, when, or if they are called into play, and the particular form in which they manifest themselves, will be in response or reaction to the conditions of the corporate environment. The strengths developed in childhood will be further developed in articulation with and reaction to experiences in the workplace. Many of these strengths are values orientations and values often are called on to surface or may be solidified, reinforced, and transformed through social interaction.[1]

Like Robert Hill, Stinnett (1983) based his research on the conviction that we must first identify those characteristics of strong families to prescribe remedies for those families in need of strengthening. He identified certain traits found consistently among strong families. These include mutual appreciation, time spent together, commitment, good communication, religion, and a constructive approach to crisis.

Hall and King (1982) added yet more strengths to the list: participation in kin-structured networks, elastic households, resilient children, egalitarian two-parent relationships, and steadfast optimism. Curran (1983) asked members of the clergy, educators, and counselors who work with families to identify what constitutes a healthy family. The sizable number of professional books and journal articles published recently, particularly since 1980, illustrate the growing interest among scholars in this relatively new focus on family strengths (see Berretta, 1982; Hurd, 1995; Littlejohn-Blake & Darling, 1993; Olson & McCubbin, 1983, 1989; Ronnau, 1993; Stinnett, 1980, 1981, 1983;

Vance, 1989; Walsh, 1982). Indeed, we can say that the issue of family strengths is a central concern within the field of family social science.

THE CASE FOR AN INTERACTIVE MODEL
OF FAMILY STRENGTH

A portion of the research has focused on a search for discrete entities—that is, finite characteristics that can be universally identified as marriage and family strengths (Curran, 1983; Hall & King, 1982; McCubbin & McCubbin, 1988; Otto, 1962, 1975; Sawin, 1979; Schultz, 1991; Spanier, 1976; Stinnett, 1983; Vance, 1989). Some researchers argue that a family must have all of the identified strengths; others use a linear rating scale to determine which families are more or less healthy.

Parsonian models in the literature have focused on family functioning on both the instrumental (material) and the expressive (socioemotional) dimensions (see Parsons & Bales, 1955). They assert that family strengths are those traits that are functional to the maintenance of the family system by enabling it to meet the needs of its members. Parsons's work suggests, however, that the nuclear family structure is the most likely to be "functional," and exemplifies a functional family on the basis of a traditional gender role division of labor.

A few researchers, most notably Robert Hill, regard black family strengths as survival adaptations. His work remains highly applicable and is refreshing to the extent that it suggests a relationship between the strengths a people possesses and the experiences that it has encountered historically. His model remains stagnant, however, in its allusion to a monotypical black experience, and to how the strengths he identified adapt, manifest, and transform themselves anew in response to the more contemporary sources of stress for today's black families such as those experienced in the corporate environment.[2]

Also significant among advances in family strengths research important to mention here is the work of Olson and McCubbin (1983, 1989) and the Circumplex Model, including their use, in particular, of the Family Adaptability and Cohesion Evaluation Scales—FACES and FACES II. Although a modified version of FACES II, a family self-report instrument, has been used with some success among African American families, application to African American families has been extremely limited (K. Fitterer, personal communication, October 8, 1996).

In short, although some researchers have focused on specific non-traditional nuclear family forms such as step and blended families (Visher & Visher, 1983) and single-parent-headed families (Hanson, 1986), many of the existing models are often best suited to the traditional nuclear family structure. Many of these models view family needs as universals and therefore assume the existence of a universal set of family strengths that will assist all families. Existing models tend to ignore cultural differences that will affect what an individual family needs. They do not consider the sociocultural milieu in which any given family system is embedded. Those that do are not dynamic enough to take into account all of the influences acting on families.

What is needed, then, is a more dynamic approach to the study and a definition of family strengths. This is certainly not to say that the existing approaches are not important. Rather, I am suggesting the need to build from these existing models an interactive approach that proceeds from a given family's needs and recognizes that such needs are determined in part by the particular context of the family. Such an approach should not obscure the possibility that there may be certain characteristics that all families would do well to have but it does suggest that each trait be considered in context, for example, within the family's environment. Such an approach would also concede that what could be defined as a strength in one situation would not be defined as such in another. There are similarities among families; however, there are also vast differences in background, experiences, preferences, and needs that must be taken into account to effect a more meaningful discussion of family strengths.

Such a discussion must take into account the fact that any consideration of family strengths goes hand in hand with one of family stress. Strengths and stresses may appear to be at opposite ends of the spectrum; however, their interrelationship is important for us to understand. Just as we have said that what makes a particular family strong is specific to that family, so it can be argued that the stresses a family experiences are unique to it, too. We need to consider the resources a given family needs to combat the stressors that it is likely to face or that it regularly faces. We need to ask, What strengths does this family need/have to manage the particular stressors it faces and to maintain its health?

Because all U.S. families, regardless of race, share certain human needs and participate to some extent in U.S. cultural life, we can allow ourselves to talk in a general way about some of the categories of strengths that most families need.[3] We must, however, keep in mind that there are as many variations in the family experience as there are families. Therefore, the quantity and type of strength a family needs will vary from family to family. Some families will need an abundance of a certain category of strength or several categories of strengths, to be considered healthy. Others may not. Although families need to exhibit some degree of strength on several dimensions, a high rating on a particular strength may not be necessary for all families to be truly healthy. There can be no universal law then regarding which, how much, and how many strengths are necessary to make for a healthy family.

We are now ready to answer the question we asked previously about what constitutes a strong family. A strong family is one that has adequate and appropriate resources to meet the circumstances, stressful or otherwise, that it is likely to face. In deciding whether or not a given family is strong or healthy, we must ask the question: Does this family have the resources it needs to maintain itself in a healthy fashion?

I will conclude this discussion on stress and family strengths by offering some direction for theory building. Suggestions for the future direction of family strengths research will be offered in the final chapter.

There appear to be two elements essential to a viable definition of family strengths. First, there are some things that would be defined as strengths in any family context, such as "good" communication, affectional bonds, concern for the well-being of family members, and so forth. Second, and I would argue more important, that strengths are best viewed in light of the experiences or potential stressors that families are likely to face. More specifically, strengths are best viewed in light of a given family's categorical and individual context, on the basis of such factors as race, class, family structure, and that family's particular life circumstances and experiences. Certainly, because any given family's circumstances and experiences will change over the course of the family life span, so, too, will the specific strengths that it will need for survival and wellness. From this point, I would like to offer the following definition of family strengths. Family strengths might be defined as the variety of resources including good communication, strong affectional bonds, ability to perform family roles flexibly, commitment to family unity, ability to provide primary group satisfaction and support, and any other qualities or abilities that promote family health and well-being prophylactically, potentially, and functionally.

In the next chapter, I will explain how the research was conducted including a discussion of the materials used, the data employed, and how they were drawn.

Notes

1. Both Durkheim (1964) and Goffman (1959) suggest this notion, although in somewhat different ways, in their treatment of ceremonies and rituals.

2. Although Hill's model of identified family strengths is far from exhaustive of the strengths that black families may possess and lacks dynamics, it still is extremely useful as a general assessment of a limited, although significant, body of strengths that are historically specific to African American families.

3. Theoreticians and practitioners must take special care not to conceive of only a finite universe of family strengths. It may not be possible to anticipate all of the traits and characteristics that may function for a given family as a strength. I will still argue that to a very great extent family strengths are most accurately determined in the context of each individual family.

3

How the Research Was Done

Methods, Materials,
and Sources of Data

The objective of this investigation was to identify the sources of stress and strengths of black corporate managers and their families, and to explore the nature of their experiences. This chapter will focus on the data needed, the tools and techniques used in gathering them, the sources of data, and the selection of the sample.

The data for this study were collected on the basis of in-depth personal interviews and written questionnaires. Interviews were conducted with corporate managers, some of their spouses, and less formal interviews were conducted with the children of corporate managers. Interviews with managers and their spouses ranged from 50 minutes to 2.5 hours in length. The modal time length of interviews was 1.5 hours. Interviews were audiotape-recorded. The eight-part interview questionnaire (see Appendix A for content and organization) contained both open- and close-ended questions. Questions about educational attainment, job status and status mobility, career aspirations and expectations, family of origin, personal and family success, leisure time activities, political party affiliation and views on the ERA and affirmative action, work demands and relocation, performance and treatment in the workplace, perceptions of racism in the corporate world, friendship and social networks, family support, work history of women in the family, church attendance and religiosity, achievement aspirations, domestic chores and child-rearing responsibilities, and personal and work role

TABLE 3.1 Sample Breakdown by Method of Data Collection

Respondents	Method	N
Managers	Personal interview	187
Managers	Self-administered questionnaire only	4
Spouses	Personal interview	38
Spouses	Self-administered questionnaire only	44
Spouses	Self-administered questionnaire and telephone interview	20
Children	Personal interview	33

support from spouse were asked. Although in most cases the interview process, including the questions asked, was fairly standard, in some instances the interviewer probed to bring out more in-depth and detailed responses to questions. Of all the managers contacted to be interviewed, most were enthusiastic about participating in the project and only one declined. Most managers were interviewed in their offices; most spouses were interviewed at home. In total, 187 managers were interviewed (see Table 3.1). Data from managers were drawn via written questionnaires and returned by mail in only four cases.

Of the spouses, 38 were personally interviewed. Of the remainder, 100 were mailed written questionnaires that were returned at a rate of 64%. In total, 64 questionnaires were returned. In several cases ($N = 20$), telephone interviews were conducted as a follow-up with completed questionnaires. Children were included in the sample and were interviewed on the basis of whether or not opportunities to do so presented themselves.

With two exceptions, all of the interviews were conducted by the author, who has extensive experience and training in the interview process. In the two cases of exception, interviews were conducted by a sociology doctoral candidate who holds a master's degree in survey research and who was intimately knowledgeable about the project. She conducted these interviews on occasions when it was impossible for the author to keep interview appointments.

There is a significant advantage in using only one interviewer for the entire study. First and foremost, interviewer bias, in some senses, would remain consistent from interview to interview. That is, we would expect that the interviewer's phrasing of questions, probings, intonations, and personal deportment would remain relatively constant from one interview to the next. An additional advantage was that the interviewer's race was the same as that of the respondents, which may have increased the latter's comfort level and candidness in responding to questions. Kidder (1981) states that blacks frequently will respond to questions in an interview situation differently if the interviewer is white versus black. Interviews were conducted in a relaxed, informal tone and there was no reason to expect any level of discomfort or lack of candidness to exist due to the researcher's identity. The backup interviewer was of the same sex and race as the principal interviewer.

Specific question areas included in both the interview and written self-administered questionnaires focused on personal and family background, corporate demands, work environment, community (the African American community in a social, not geographic, sense), political outlook (party affiliation, their opinions about affirmative action and the ERA, the future of blacks in the United States), personal and family strengths, spousal involvement/expectations, family stress, and interpersonal relationships. Some of these areas were further subdivided to address a range of concerns in these areas. Interviews with children were much more loosely focused and primarily examined friendships, race perception, racial identity and prejudice, and were conducted either on a one-to-one basis or in groups.

DESCRIPTION OF THE SAMPLE

The sample was composed of three categories of subjects including black corporate managers, their spouses (mostly wives), and the children of black corporate managers. It consisted of 191 mostly middle- and upper-middle-level managers, but also included a few first-line and some upper-level managers, most of whom live and/or work in the New York-Connecticut-New Jersey tri-state area. Also included were selected respondents from San Francisco; Los Angeles; Washington, D.C.; Cincinnati, and Atlanta to examine the national representativeness of the sample. A total of 102 spouses, all but 4 of whom were wives, were interviewed or responded to questionnaires administered by mail. The sample of children totaled 33. It was decided that the N for both spouses and children needed to be neither larger, because this was a qualitative

TABLE 3.2 Breakdown of Sample by Type of Respondent

Respondents	N	Total
Managers, male	142	
Managers, female	49	
Total managers		191
Spouses, wives	98	
Spouses, husbands	4	
Total spouses		102
Children		33

TABLE 3.3 Marital Status of Managers by Sex

	Male	Female	Total
Married	141	17	158
Single—never married	—	12	12
Divorced	1	20	21
Total	142	49	191

study, nor as large as that of the managers. A partial rationale for including a larger number of managers was to pick up the variation of responses, if any, that might be an artifact of corporate culture. (This is further discussed in the following pages.) All respondents, by virtue of the employment status of one, if not both, heads of households, can be described as middle or upper-middle class (see Table 3.2).

The breakdown of the sample of managers by sex was 142 males and 49 females. All of the male managers were presently married, with the exception of one who was divorced. For most, it was their first marriage. Two fifths (39%) of the female managers were divorced, a quarter (25%) single, and only slightly more than a third (36%) were presently married (see Table 3.3).[1]

Most of the spouses of the managers in the sample were employed (88%), the majority of them (62%) full-time. Most were employed in the field of education, mainly as teachers, counselors, and learning specialists. Some held corporate, including managerial, positions. The spouses included in the sample were married to managers in the sample, although they did not necessarily have to be spouses of respondent managers because few questions were analyzed "within family"—there were only a few issues where I was interested in the differences or similarities in impressions between spouses, within couples (e.g., husbands' assessments of the extent of their contributions to performing domestic tasks versus wives' assessment of their husbands' contributions).

The children included in the study ranged in age from 8 to 14. The modal age was 12. The sample included nearly equal proportions of males and females. Most were enrolled in private schools. Most appeared to be bright and articulate. One third were children of respondent managers.

All managers, with very few exceptions (3), had some college education (188), and approximately 75% were college graduates (145). Among the college graduates, well over half (84) had completed some graduate work, and quite a few had graduate degrees (73). Of their spouses, all but one had some college education; nearly 75% were college graduates (138), among whom nearly half had graduate degrees (67).

Managers ranged in age from 31 to 60 with the mean age for female managers being 39, and for male managers 41. Of all the managers, 90% had children—17% had one child, 55% had two children, and 18% had three or more. Managers' salaries ranged from $35,000 to more than $200,000 per year.

Managers had been employed by their present companies from 2 years to 34 years. The average length of tenure was 14 years. Respondents had come to choose corporate life either through contact with corporate recruiters in college and graduate school, because they enjoyed their business courses in school, because corporate jobs potentially offer high salaries, or because opportunities were made available to them. Many chose their specific companies because they are reputed to offer good career development opportunities for blacks compared with other companies.

Respondents were not from caste-privileged or elite families as might be anticipated. Three fourths of the respondents were from working-class backgrounds; about one fourth were from middle-class backgrounds. Managers described themselves as "good" to "very good" students, and several of them ranked in the top 10% of their high school graduating class, college graduating classes, or both. A few described themselves as "okay."

A DESCRIPTION OF THE COMPANIES

Respondents were drawn (with one exception) from eight Fortune 100 companies. Most of the corporations can be described as specializing in office information systems and manufacturing, but also included were a food products company and a petrochemical company. Several of these corporations are reputed as being among the most socially progressive with respect to their interest in worker needs, worker satisfaction, and employee assistance programs—particularly in the context of managing a diverse workforce. All eight companies in the sample are headquartered in the northeastern part of the United States. The sample was drawn from among the most financially successful U.S. corporations to ensure inclusion of some of the best, brightest, and most successful blacks in corporate America. This enabled us to see if black managers, even at the level of those who have the best personal and professional credentials and have been most successful, have the array of problems that this research explores.

HOW THE SAMPLE WAS CHOSEN

Respondents were chosen on the basis of personal contacts and through referrals. The data were not drawn from a random sample. The researcher began with a list of black managers in one corporation obtained from a former president of the company's black employees' organization. In another instance, a personal friend of the researcher, employed by another corporation, developed a list of names of managers who were interested in the study and were willing to participate. In other instances, personal acquaintances of the researcher in various companies were contacted who offered suggestions as to who might be contacted for an interview. Several respondents made referrals of coworkers, acquaintances, friends, and relatives in their own and other companies.[2] The pool of prospective respondents grew as referrals kept coming. In turn, the sample size kept growing. Managers wanted to tell their story. The criteria used in including prospective respondents (managers) in the sample included that they be employed in management positions in Fortune 100 companies, and that they contributed to the diversity of the total sample by sex, age, tenure in the company, and level of management. Multiple corporations were included to increase the chances that what respondents were saying was somewhat representative of the experiences and sentiments of black corporate managers generally rather than an artifact of a particular corporate culture and experience. A sizable N in each company was drawn to ensure diversity within the companies by the same variables of sex, age, tenure in the company, and level of management desired within the total sample. It was, however, not deemed necessary that this diversity be replicated in exactly the same numbers or proportions in each company. The sample size was thought to be sufficient when this diversity was achieved.

ANALYSIS

This research was conceptualized as an exploratory study. A qualitative approach to the study of black corporate family life was taken, enabling the researcher to listen to the voices of managers and their families as they expressed their views and sentiments and described their experiences. For the stated reasons, the sample size is larger than might be considered usual for a qualitative study. Because the sample is not a random one and also because this is largely an "inductive," hypothesis-discovering exploratory study analysis, techniques are primarily descriptive rather than quantitative. Because of the methodological limitations of the sampling techniques used, rigorous quantitative analysis is not warranted and is deemed inappropriate by the researcher. Rosenblatt, Karis, and Powell (1995) suggest that rigorous statistical analysis with nonrandom samples is "meaningless" (p. 23). For the same reason, even the use of the simplest of descriptive statistics is limited. Rather, I will offer some general impressions of experience relative to the particulars of corporate black family life that are explored in this study. Furthermore, on initial examination of the data, it was evident that responses did not vary on the basis of the variables by which the sample was loosely stratified. Therefore, it did not appear that quantitative analysis would be particularly useful but that a more qualitative approach would be more interesting and informative.

In addition, by using a qualitative approach, this research endeavors to pull into balance the existing body of literature on African American families. Demos (1990) points to the overwhelmingly pervasive use of quantitative versus qualitative methodology in studying African American families. Littlejohn-Blake and Darling (1993) argue that the existing body of literature does not capture the full flavor of African American family life and, in fact, "skews" our understanding of it because of the paucity of qualitative research endeavors, which are able to provide "a more richly detailed" body of data. They point to the value of adding qualitative research efforts to the field. Littlejohn-Blake and Darling assert that "qualitative designs facilitate an understanding of the subjects' point of view, provide the researcher with flexibility in studying social life, and are particularly suited to the discovery of new ideas." Ambert, Adler, Adler, and Detzner (1995) observed that only 1.9% of those studies published in the *Journal of Marriage and Family* in recent years (1989-1994) were qualitative, suggesting a paucity of published qualitative research in the field of family studies in general. In concurrence with Demos's, Littlejohn-Blake and Darling's, and Ambert et al.'s (1995) observations and assertions, taking a qualitative approach to this project was seen as potentially both insightful and invaluable.

The quotes included in the text of the book do not reflect analysis of only some of the data. Rather, those cases quoted in fact represent and are characteristic of mean and modal responses. They do not reflect merely individual or peculiarly poignant quotes, but are clear articulations and "summarizations" of the sentiments shared by other respondents in the sample. (As an example, most managers reported that family, especially mothers, encouraged them in their educational pursuits. The quote included in Chapter 4 in response to questions regarding parental encouragement in educational pursuits, "I owe a lot to my mother's push!," was selected for inclusion from other similar responses including the following: "I couldn't have done it without moms." "My mother was always there behind us." "Yes, my mother.")

What Is the Power of This Study to Inform Us About Black Families in Corporate America?

Because the sample is not a random one, the question arises—of what population is it representative? I recognize the lack of a random sample as a weakness in the research design of the study restricting its power to generalize to the larger population. Studies employing interview data, however, typically do not draw from random samples. A stratified random sample drawn from each of the companies by the variables selected for inclusion in the samples (sex, age, tenure, and level of management) would offer an improvement. To account for this weakness, a larger sample size than is perhaps usual for a qualitative study was used so that the sample group might begin to approach representativeness of the total population of black corporate managers employed in Fortune 100 companies and their families. As was previously mentioned, such a large N was also used to allow for a sizable enough representation of respondents from each of the various companies included in the study. Both the large sample size, as well as the multiple number of companies from which the sample was drawn, should enable us to make reasonably accurate broad inferences about the total population of black managers. Furthermore, the large N, and especially the high level of consistency of responses in repeated applications of the interview instrument, drawn from several different companies, suggests the possibility and the likelihood that the data drawn for this study are a valid and reliable source of data that informs us generally about black managers in corporate America and their families.

With respect to the strengths of the study—although there was some flexibility in procedure from N to N to assist the flow of the interview and to maintain respondent interest (an advantage of qualitative methodology and the interview technique), the interview procedure was relatively standard and did not vary dramatically to avoid any threat to generalizability. Questions were consistently worded from interview to interview. This standardization of questions should also function to increase validity. Questions of validity and reliability are different and of lesser importance in qualitative studies than would be the case in those studies that are strictly quantitative. Validity and reliability in qualitative studies such as this, whose data are composed primarily of self reports, have to be assessed differently than in quantitative ones largely because of the reliance on respondent's perceptions and assessments. In this study, triangulation was possible because of the large sample size (as well as the inclusion of more than one type of data collection method as was the case with managers' wives and the use of self-administered questionnaires and personal interviews)—researcher perceptions could be rechecked from case to case (see Brewer & Hunter, 1989). This functioned to strengthen validity.

Although this study cannot be viewed as definitive because of its methodological weaknesses, it should be considered important and relevant to the broader population from which it was drawn. At the very least, it strongly suggests possible realities of black corporate family life and can be used as a basis for generating hypotheses for further research.

Assessment of How the Research Was Done

Ambert et al. (1995), in their review article of qualitative research in family studies, suggest criteria that describe and provide guidelines for evaluating qualitative research. They elaborate on the goals and procedures of qualitative research, the connections between epistemologies and methods and theory and literature, and they address issues of analysis, validity, and reliability. The following discussion speaks to and flows out of some of the issues raised in their review. Specifically, I would like to address

- the value of qualitative research in understanding and explaining behavior;
- discovery as a goal of research;
- the linkages of epistemology and theory to methodology;
- identity of the researcher vis-à-vis her or his subjects, and subject matter;
- contributions of the research to empirical knowledge;
- support for using qualitative methods; and
- what this research will offer.

So little has been done by way of qualitative family studies. Ambert et al. (1995) suggest, and I concur, that we are missing so many of the "real stories" that quantitative methods just cannot discover—how and why people behave as they do and how to give meaning to their experiences. To accomplish this, as is consistent with qualitative methods, open-ended questions in in-depth interviews were used in this research.

Consistent with much of that body of qualitative research, this study is one of discovery versus verification. Although this work does include some hypothesis testing, it has hypothesis discovery as its main goal.

In this research, epistemology is tied to methodology. This is true both in how the methodology was decided on, as well as the types of specific questions that were asked. My assumptions about the world regarding the persistence of racism, and about the worldview or spirit of African

American families, both guided the formulation and choice of questions, the hypotheses chosen for the research, the appropriateness of collecting data using the interview technique, and the absolute richness of data that can be collected in an open-ended questionnaire, in-person interview format on the subjects under study. Accordingly, we can best understand individual and family behavior of the type explored in this study using the kind of methodology that was employed. Consistent with the Chicago School epistemology, I entered the world of corporate managers (their places of business) and their families (their homes), and attempted to create a comfortable and relaxed atmosphere (e.g., through body language, verbal gestures, cordiality, and openness) spending relatively nonstructured, open-ended time asking questions and from there formulating hypotheses. In the Chicago School tradition, both theory and hypotheses emerged from the data (Collins & Makowsky, 1993). Also included in this tradition is the symbolic interactionist perspective, which emphasizes the importance of both verbal and nonverbal gestures in the communication process (Blumer, 1969). The interactionist perspective also guided this investigation both philosophically, in my research orientation, projecting the importance of nonverbal communication in completing our understanding of human motivation, sentiments, and behavior directing me to the methodological techniques that were chosen, and, actually, enriching and enlivening the data that were collected. (See Prus, 1996 for a discussion of the importance of tying epistemology, theory, and methodology to the real-world lives of the subjects we study.)

As a researcher, I felt particularly well suited to the nature of this investigation. It is to my racial and social-class background that I refer. We know that one's subjective understandings of the social world are influenced by one's position in that world. Thus, the approach to research and the interpretation of data are socially situated and occur within the context of the researcher's experience. This experience is influenced by race, class, and gender identities. In a very real sense, my personal background identities of class and race oriented me to the realities of the experiences of the respondents. I posit this as a methodological strength of the study.

If qualitative research, like other forms of research, should be evaluated on the basis of "whether it makes a substantive contribution to empirical knowledge and/or advances theory," as Ambert et al. (1995,

p. 883) suggest, this research should be positively assessed. It gives voice to those who previously were little heard in the literature and asks a new set of questions. Furthermore, this study is linked to the literature and theory at various stages, it prods the theory in new directions, and it contributes to our knowledge of a specific population of families that have been all but neglected in the literature.

A more dynamic process of analysis is more usual in and better lends itself to qualitative versus quantitative study—another reason why this method was chosen for this particular study. Preliminary analyses of data took place as data were being collected. The strong trends and themes that emerged and grew (strengthened) as more and more data were collected caused me to question whether this was an artifact of sampling from companies that were too similar, or a result of the "snowball" technique used in selecting the sample. In addressing these concerns and limitations, the sample size grew to unusual proportions for a qualitative study (although the guidelines for sample size in qualitative studies are only general) as I added new companies to rule out the effect of organizational culture and the possible effect of sampling among members of the same social network (although this was not likely to be the case) due to the snowball method of sampling. Although increasing the sample size had the benefit of allaying my initial concerns about the trends that emerged from the data by virtue of the fact that they persisted and strengthened, on the downside I am left with a sample size that to some may seem unwieldy or even inappropriate for qualitative analysis. Despite this catch-22 or the paradox inherent in this situation, however, I remain faithful and committed to the value of qualitative research and analysis and am unseduced by what might be perceived by some as the need to now shift gears and add on more quantitative analysis simply because the sample size got bigger (albeit for a good reason) than is typical or necessary for good qualitative investigation. Rather, on the positive side, increasing the sample size enhanced the validity of the data by establishing a pattern or trend and allowing it more likely to be generalizable to the larger population of black corporate managers from the variety of Fortune 100 companies from which it was drawn and thereby more representative. (A sample must be relatively large if it is to be representative of an entire population.)

From this study, I will provide the reader with summaries of the data by way of simple quantifications, categories, graphic presentations, verbal assessments and generalizations, selected respondent profiles, and, in particular, the respondents' own words. It is in the richness of the quotes and profiles of the respondents that the "meat" of the data will be found. It is in these ways, but especially through the latter, that I hope to convey the range and array of sentiments, emotions, values, and motivations that characterize the respondents and bring them to life for the reader and enable the reader to feel their joys, concerns, obstacles, and strengths.

The next part of the book focuses on the substantive topics included in this research. We will begin with a presentation of selected data.

Notes

1. The marital status "divorced" was much more pervasive among the female versus male respondents in the sample. The data collected do not include information regarding when those previously married respondents divorced. Although a few respondents did mention that they divorced while employed as corporate managers, most gave no indication as to whether or not the divorce came before or after they ascended to the corporate managerial ranks. One female respondent felt, however, that her career success and mobility to the rank of manager was threatening to her husband, causing a strain on their marriage, and ultimately led to their divorce. It would be interesting to know, and I suggest that further research efforts explore, whether either high levels of wife's career success or the demands of corporate managerial employment are causal factors of divorce among black female corporate managers.

2. Although the "snowball" method of sampling employed suggests that because some of the managers were acquainted with other managers included in the sample, similarity of responses to some questions asked in the interview could at least partially be influenced by network overlap. This might be possible in some instances; however, it would not be overall. It appeared that, with very few exceptions, although some managers were professionally acquainted, they were not socially connected. Most respondents were not friends of other respondents, and, in those cases in which they were, those friendships in most instances did not extend outside of the job and did not include managers' families.

PART II

The Data

Presentation of Selected Data

This section of the book (Chapters 4-10) will focus on the issues and questions raised in Chapter 1 (see the section titled The Problem at Hand) that are central to this research. But, before moving on to the findings on some of the more substantive issues of relevance, let us begin with some findings that offer a general profile of the respondents. Specifically, let us look at factors related to their success, selected political views, and leisure time. Please be reminded that these data are drawn from self-reports (as are all of the data that inform this study) and, therefore, assessments of various traits, characteristics, and behaviors are highly subjective. Perceptions of self, in some cases, may be skewed in a negative direction due to rigid personal standards, variables that factor into the construction of perceptions, or both, or, in other cases, overly flattering perceptions or more of a representation of how one would like to perceive of self. We will revisit these notions and discuss the significance of self perceptions before we begin the next chapter.

BLACK MANAGERS AND SUCCESS

One of the unique characteristics of the participants in this study that distinguishes them among blacks and among other Americans is their high level of occupational success. Therefore, several items contained in the interview questionnaire addressed this point from a variety of angles. Nearly all managers viewed their level of success as greater than that of their siblings (136, $N = 191$), and greater than that of those with whom they grew up (187, $N = 191$). They attributed their success to personal style, being a self-starter, their value systems, and parental encouragement. All but one ($N = 191$) felt that parents had very definitely encouraged them in their educational pursuits and in general, and that this was a major factor contributing to their success. Nearly all respondents (168, $N = 191$) had mentors in corporate America, most of whom were white, although some were black. Most viewed having a mentor(s) as important to one's success.

When asked if they considered themselves to be successful, most male managers (139, $N = 191$) responded "yes," but several female managers responded "no" or only "somewhat." The responses of males to this question seemed to be consistent with previous research findings that male perceptions of success are based on their perceptions of adequacy in the provider role as based on income (see Taylor et al., 1988). For females, however, self-assessments of success seemed to be more tied to cultural phenomena and traditional gender role prescriptions, which tie female success to their domestic roles as wives and mothers. This seems to be an obstacle to perception of self as successful, particularly for those women who were childless, single, or divorced. Furthermore, the complex "juggling act" of trying to do all three jobs as worker, wife, and mother well may prevent some married women with children from feeling totally competent and completely successful.

RESPONDENTS' POLITICAL OUTLOOK

In voicing their political outlook, respondents were quite expressive. Although their responses varied somewhat in intensity, the tone of responses was very similar with no appreciable differences by age or sex. There were some differences by age suggesting that younger managers, in some cases, were more politically conservative than older managers. Research with more of a specific focus on this issue would be required, however, to make more definitive and informative statements on this subject.

Subject's political party affiliation was overwhelmingly Democratic (187, $N = 191$), with few deviations. Two respondents were Independents, one was Republican, and one had no formal affiliation. Most of the companies for which respondents worked had a black or minority employees' organization. Almost 95% of more than 150 respondents who worked for such corporations participated in these organizations and were active participants and supporters. Most of those who did not participate said they could not do so due to family obligations—most of these were mothers who were single parents.

When asked about affirmative action, managers responded strongly in favor of it. The few negative statements expressed regarding these policies and programs were that they cause some whites to assume that blacks are not qualified for their jobs and had to be hired to fill employment quotas, and that these policies now work for white women, sometimes to the detriment of blacks and other minorities. One subject seemed to sum up the sentiment of most of the managers in his response: "Affirmative action is good and necessary. Without it we wouldn't have gotten this far." When asked if affirmative action was still needed today, another respondent said, "It's still needed to keep people honest." Other responses included the following: "I'm very strongly in favor of affirmative action. I feel it's essential and I feel it's a real setback that these programs have been cut." "It's very definitely needed, but it's gone! Some of us will survive, but it will be rough!"

Views on the subject of the ERA and equal rights for women were also strong and positive. Nearly all managers (153, $N = 191$) were in favor of these issues, although a few (37, $N = 191$) felt policies and programs for women's rights were unnecessary. Some managers responded negatively, saying that blacks have more of an issue. One (male) manager responded, "Women have done very well in corporate America. They're the ones for whom affirmative action has really paid off." Another responded, "There's an 'old girls' network in this company, and it's strong!" Yet another said, "The sheet has no zipper" (referring to the sheets worn by the Ku Klux Klan and the zipper on men's trousers). "White women can be just as racist as white men." Although nearly all female respondents were in favor of policies that promote women's rights, most of them said they felt more strongly about affirmative action policies and programs for blacks than they did toward similar policies and programs for women and felt they are more necessary. One woman responded, when asked about obstacles to women's success in corporate America, "There are too many narrow-minded men who see a woman's place as in the kitchen. This prohibits the success of women in the corporation."

On the subject of the future of blacks in America, although many were positive in their outlook, they, too, were not without fears and reservations.

Many managers began their responses with one- or two-word descriptors including "good," "bright," "questionable," "less optimistic," "hard," "pessimistic." They went on to say that they had concerns about such things as racism, black youth and drugs, teen pregnancy, school dropout rates, and what the future holds for their own children as blacks in the United States. The following responses are reflective of the mix of sentiment that ranges from positive to cautious within all of the individuals who were interviewed.

Question: How would you describe the future of blacks in the United States?

Good, bright, but we've got a long way to go.

We've got to be careful. We could be in trouble. We still have to be better (than whites).

Well, we'll be okay. We'll survive. But it will be rough for us especially, and rough for everyone else. We're always on the bottom. We will have to help ourselves.

A mixed bag due to poverty and ignorance. The underclass. But there will be lots of blacks who economically will be in the mainstream.

MANAGERS AND THEIR FAMILIES' LEISURE TIME

The leisure time activities that managers and their families engage in range from cooking to music, with reading, travel, and photography being the most popular, respectively. They also enjoy antiques/collectibles, gardening, electronics, movies, sewing, camping, drawing, watching television, getting together with friends, professional associations, church, and child-centered activities. One respondent said that he had no time for leisure activities. Many actively enjoy sports with tennis being the most popular, but also mentioned were fishing, running, golf, skiing, and racquetball. All managers and their families, with one exception, enjoy annual vacations—some two to three yearly. Vacation plans often include visits with relatives, as well as travel to places that included Martha's Vineyard, Vail, Myrtle Beach, parts of California and Florida, Puerto Rico, the Virgin Islands, the Bahamas, Bermuda, Jamaica and other parts of the Caribbean, Canada, Mexico, and parts of Europe. The opportunity to connect with family and the availability of sun and beach are high priorities in planning vacations.

When asked what they spent their extra money on, the first response of most was to laugh and exclaim, "What extra money?!" But many of them found some money to spend on things such as travel, clothing, dining out, specialty foods and fine wines, theater, jewelry, art/paintings, savings/investments, movies, music, church, hobbies, recreation, entertainment, books, sports events, cars, house, spouse, and their relatives. On average, these black corporate managerial families live in well-appointed homes, are well dressed, shop in fine stores, and enjoy gourmet food. Their favorite ice cream is Häagen Dazs® (60.4%, $N = 191$).

The Value of Self-Reports

The question arises as to how much faith to put in "facts" drawn from self reports. What is the validity of respondents' personal testimony about the facts of their lives and the causes of their actions? By way of example, do we trust that family was a major factor contributing to their success, because they tell us it was? Do we conclude that some of these single black female managers are not successful because they do not consider themselves to be—even if more objective criteria would suggest otherwise? The pros and cons of subjective versus objective research are complex and difficult to sort out. On one hand, objective data are absolutely crucial and of key importance in our understanding of social causation. But, at the same time, we also need to pay attention to what people tell us. We need to put some credence in self-assessments and subjective understanding. Certainly such an argument is a major tenet of the symbolic interactionist approach (see Blumer, 1969). Similarly, Collins and Makowsky (1993) posit in their description of the aims of the Chicago School that, "Social life must be seen from the inside, as people actually experience it." W. I. Thomas (Collins & Makowsky, 1993), a pioneering member of that school, many years ago said, "If men define situations as real, they are real in their consequences." Individuals' perceptions of reality often influence their actions. In accordance with the Thomas theorem, which the quote has come to be called, objective facts in some cases may not be so important as perception of fact in their causal effect on actions. Believing that family is a major contributor to success, whether it was or not, is likely to color one's image and ideal of family and thus influence one's own actions toward and esteem for family in response. This would appear to be the case as we look ahead to Chapter 4 and the family strength of supportive kinship networks. In the case of single female managers' perceptions of success, the belief that one is not successful is likely to affect one's self-esteem and may cause one to expend an exorbitant amount of energy seeking fulfillment and success by chasing the American cultural dream of female success and fulfillment through marriage and motherhood. This will be explored in Chapter 5. Subjective research, such as in the case of research based on self-reports, can constitute a highly valid source of data informing of actions as well as people's possible motivations to actions.

The next chapter will focus on the sources of stress and the strengths of black families in corporate America.

4

What the Findings of This Study Reveal About Corporate Family Stress and Black Family Strengths

Even if I don't need their support it's extremely important to me to know that I can count on their support.

—W. Timothy Willis, 47-year-old male manager

As social scientists query, explore, and identify the sources of stress for any particular group of families, the question, "What are the strengths that bolster these families?" might logically follow. This chapter examines this study's data in these two related areas. It will look at the sources of stress for black corporate families and identify the strengths of the black corporate families in this study. A major focus in this treatment of strengths will be the five black family strengths identified by Robert Hill (1971). Because I agree with Hill, despite the shortcomings of his model (discussed in Chapter 2, this volume), that the strengths he identified have a unique meaning for black families in the United States, I have chosen to use his five strengths as the criteria for measuring the health and success of the black corporate families interviewed in this study. I do not mean to suggest, as Hill did not, that these are the only strengths to be found among black families, and this notion should become clear as one reads on, but have chosen to focus on these strengths because they are special and important to the black experience. The work of Hill provides us with a good starting point for the identification of strengths in black corporate families. The reader should come away from this chapter with the understanding that, "This is what stresses black corporate families, and this is what strengthens them."

All corporate managers, regardless of race, are subject to the stresses that result from long hours of work, out-of-town travel, the pressure of deadlines, and competitiveness in the workplace. But, as this investigation will show, for black managers and their families, the stress inherent in the corporate way of life is compounded by their ongoing experience of racism.

In light of the findings of previous researchers contained in Chapter 2, let us examine the data this study has generated through interviews with black corporate managers and their families.

What This Study Reveals About Stress in Black Corporate Families

Although review of the general literature on corporate stress reveals that research has centered on family work-related stress, the findings of this study indicate that for black managers, the workplace is, in fact, a source of greater stress. In other words, although both black managers and white managers are subject to stress at work and at home, black managers experience additional stress in the workplace and less of the more typical type of family work-related stress. (An added component to family work-related stress, in addition to workplace stress, which families face especially in connection with relocation, is social racial isolation in their communities, which will be mentioned later.) Regarding less family work-related stress, let us refer back to our earlier discussion in Chapter 2 of the experience of relocation and its effects on the corporate wife. In the sample, relocation for wives did not appear to be as traumatic to sense of status and self-esteem as the literature suggests it may be for white corporate wives. This can be explained partly by the fact that the wives of black managers are more highly educated than the wives of their white counterparts (Fernandez, 1981). Thus, they are more likely to find their own avenues for self-esteem and actualization and to be more adaptable to the demands of the corporate lifestyle than the general literature would suggest. This does not mean that black corporate managers and their families are exempt from the problems of family work-related stress but rather that these problems are overshadowed by workplace stress—not only of the type experienced by white corporate managers, but a stress compounded by the elements of racism and tokenism. Both institutional and individual racism, in their subtle and not-so-subtle forms, constitute additional sources of stress for black managers. Respondents in this study stated that the experience of racism continues to be an inescapable part of being black in corporate America.

This study's finding—that the workplace is a major source of stress for black employees—confirms the findings reported in the limited literature that exists on black corporate workers. Such studies also identified racism as the root cause of this problem.

Although all the respondents in this study agreed that workplace stress outweighed family work-related stress (many, however, said they worried about the time spent away from the family and its impact on the family), many respondents did not experience the exclusion from informal work groups that Fernandez (1981) reported (see Chapter 2). Some, however, did feel that they were excluded from social gatherings with white workers. Not participating in social events disadvantages blacks because social gatherings can serve as opportunities to cement relationships with subordinates and peers who are in positions to be supportive in the workplace and who can recommend workers for assignments and promotions. Furthermore, excluding blacks from social gatherings denies whites the opportunity to get to know and become more comfortable with blacks, leaving intact the race barrier in the workplace.

Racism was experienced by respondents in this study in other ways, too. Of the total sample of managers ($N = 191$), 138 respondents stated that they were better educated than their white counterparts, and all but five reported that they were more experienced than whites employed at the same level. Black women also made these assertions comparing themselves with white women. Many felt that they would be further along in their companies if they were white and that race had been an impediment to their upward mobility in the corporate world. When asked the question directly, "Does racism persist in corporate America?," all responded with a firm or emphatic "yes."

The Strengths of Black Corporate Families

What strengths do black corporate families need to protect them from the stressors that they are likely to face? To answer this question, their sources of stress and what resources they have that function as strengths must be identified. Let us first remind ourselves about the stressors that corporate families in general and black corporate families in particular face.

It has been documented in the professional and trade literature (see Davis & Watson, 1982; Fernandez, 1981; Kanter, 1977) that the work life of corporate managers, although rewarding, can be both demanding and stressful. The demands of the workplace and the normative expectations implicit in the corporate culture have a direct impact on the employee and also funnel out to affect the employee's family. Notable among corporate demands on the worker and his or her family are long work hours and out-of-town travel. For the corporate worker, both result in time spent away from the family and a consequent lack of participation in family activities and household responsibilities. The spouse left at home has to cope not only with the emotional strain of separation from a loved one, but with the stress of having to manage family affairs alone.

But, as we have already noted in our previous discussions of stress, black corporate managers and their families face additional stress (see Figure 4.1). In particular, black corporate managers experience social isolation in the workplace. They are often the lone black manager at a particular level or in a given office. As they climb higher up the corporate ladder, the situation intensifies, especially for high-ranking black female managers. This isolation is not limited only to the workplace. Corporate blacks face isolation in their neighborhoods and communities as well. Employment as corporate managers affords them and their families a middle- to upper-middle-class lifestyle, which may include homeownership in an affluent community that is often almost all, if not exclusively, white. A certain degree of mobility is expected of most corporate managers over the span of their careers. Job relocations often require families to move to parts of the country where the black population is small or nonexistent.

Although its nature has changed in recent decades, racism persists in the corporate workplace. Whether subtle or blatant, racism may occur

Additional Stressors That Black Corporate Families Face		Corporate Demands
• Isolation in the workplace		• Long work hours
• Isolation in the neighborhood/ community	FAMILY	• Travel (both long work hours and travel mean time spent away from family, household responsibilities)
• Racism in the workplace		
• Racism in the community		

Figure 4.1. Nexus of Black Corporate Family Stress

more often on the institutional level. Individual racism also persists in our society and serves as a source of stress for blacks in the corporation. Not confined to the workplace, racism is part of the black corporate family experience closer to home. The racism confronted in communities, from neighbors, and in schools can be stressful for both adults and children.

STRENGTHS

The respondents in the sample showed many strengths, which promoted the survival and well-being of their families. They talked freely about the stress they had to cope with as part of the corporate lifestyle, and gave direct and indirect testimony about the sources of strength that support them and keep them strong. I do not mean to suggest that their problems are simple and easily solved, for they are complex and relentless, but that their strategies and resources for coping seemed to be both appropriate and effective in meeting the challenges of their experiences.

There appeared to be no truly weak families in the sample—at least not on the level at which I examined them. That is, I was unable to discern any overall weakness or identify any given family as weak in general or along the dimensions on which I examined them (including Robert Hill's 1971 black family strengths). Again, these are special families because of their income, education, level of success, and other assets.

As a general observation, most families appeared to possess many of the characteristics that researchers found consistently in healthy families. To turn to Stinnett's (1983) citing of strengths, families seemed to express a genuine appreciation for family members. They seemed concerned for and considerate of their spouse and children. They also expressed a firm commitment to the family unit. These families seem to maneuver through life keeping in mind the family's collective best interest.

The families in the sample seemed to possess, to varying degrees, all of the five traditional black family strengths identified by Robert Hill (1971; strong work orientation, adaptability of family roles, strong achievement orientation, strong religious orientation, strong kinship bonds). Because some of these traits and their expression were more significant than others, we should view them one by one. (See Appendix B for items on the interview instrument used to assess the five traditional black family strengths.)

Strong Work Orientation

It is difficult for the corporate manager to avoid the reality of long work hours and corporate travel. But, historically, it has not been unusual for black fathers to have up to two full-time jobs to make ends meet. So, for blacks, long work hours are not new. In fact, a high number of men and women in the sample reported that this had been the case with their own fathers. These families completed a multigenerational portrait that expresses a strong work orientation just as they, too, demonstrated a dedication to work through the long work hours. Of the total sample of managers ($N = 191$), 158 reported working late at least once per week; 146 reported working late more frequently; 84 reported working late four to five evenings per week. All worked jobs that required out-of-town travel ranging from four times per year (36 respondents) to four or more days per week; 84 traveled out-of-town on company business every week. Both male and female corporate managers viewed their long work hours and travel requirements in the context of their enhanced lifestyles and the improved quality of their lives, affording them a better home, better education for their children, and other comforts. Although they at times found it difficult to cope with, the wives in the sample were generally understanding of the demands for travel and long work hours placed on their husbands. A full 100% of wives were always or almost always understanding of managers' time away from home because of the job.

Adaptability of Family Roles

It can be said that historically, and for many reasons, both economic and cultural, black families socialize their children to be role flexible and to share family responsibilities (Hill, 1971). The term *role flexible* does not refer so much to gender roles as it does to a flexibility in taking on the role responsibilities of various family members, including those of the parents. This aptitude begins at an early age because children are expected to act as "parents" to younger siblings when mothers and fathers are not available. Out of necessity, as well as choice, black couples have played less traditional roles because wives shared in the breadwinning and husbands shared in the child-care functions. Although this was true historically for most black couples and across class lines, blacks in the middle class have exhibited what might be called more traditional behaviors than have the black poor or blacks in the working class. Economic necessity, which to a certain extent has motivated parents to expect these behaviors of children, must be recognized as at least a partial driver in this phenomenon. Although not all black youngsters today assume the parenting role in the same ways and to the same extent as did their counterparts in past years, some continue to assist with child rearing.

Of the respondents in the sample, 70% came from families in which women had worked and continued to work unless they were retired or deceased. Only one younger woman in the sample had a corporate father and a mother who might be categorized as a traditional, full-time, non-working corporate wife. At the time that many of the respondents were growing up, working for pay outside the household was a nontraditional behavior for U.S. women, although it was not unusual for black women who worked when the economic situation made it necessary.

Both husbands and wives described varying degrees of role flexibility in their own lives. Of the wives ($N = 98$), 67 reported that husbands shared in traditional, female-type household chores with a frequency ranging from *occasionally* to *often*. None reported that husbands never engaged in such chores. Although more than half of the husbands reported that they engaged only in male gender-proscribed household chores such as yard work, taking out the garbage, simple automobile maintenance, and household repairs, some appeared to be more egalitarian. About a quarter of husbands (total $N = 98$) had regular responsibility for nonmale gender-proscribed chores such as cooking, vacuuming, and child care, although few (18) reported anything close to an equal sharing of domestic chores, including child care. Surprisingly, there was very little difference by age in these categories of responses. Younger respondents were not much closer to gender role egalitarianism than older respondents, contrary to what we might have expected. Of the wives, 89 reported responses ranging from *sometimes* to *often* when asked how frequently they assumed the husband's household chores if he were out of town or working late. Although both sexes appear to exhibit some degree of role flexibility, wives do so to a greater extent than husbands. (See Chapter 7 for a more in-depth discussion of this subject.)

The net effect of this is that male managers especially can do their jobs without worrying about the home front. That is, they can feel comfortable, unencumbered by responsibilities at home, and able to meet the demands of their work knowing that their domestic responsibilities are being taken care of. It would appear that role flexibility is an essential support or strength for managers whose jobs and whose continued career success require large amounts of time away from home and family due to long work hours and out-of-town travel.

Strong Achievement Orientation

We might hypothesize, given the history of racism and sexism in our society, including in the corporate sector, that blacks and women would need above-average talents and skills and a high level of personal drive to be successful in corporate America. Our sample confirmed this hypothesis. The respondents seemed to have both the skills and the motivation necessary for achievement.

All but three of the respondents were college educated and, in fact, many reported that they were better educated than their white counterparts ($138, N = 191$). Because many of their parents had expected them to go to college, they grew up with this goal already set for them. They firmly attested to having been encouraged in their educational pursuits by their parents, especially their mothers. As one manager said, "I owe a lot to my mother's push!"

Nearly all respondents ($187, N = 191$) described their achievements in education, job, and income as greater than those of their childhood peers. They attributed their greater success to the fact that they are "self-starters"—they are hardworking; aggressive; highly motivated; personally driven; committed to excellence; desirous of success, monetary rewards; and willing to seize opportunities. Most of the respondents ($186, N = 191$) aspire to further promotions within or outside their present companies. Their attitude is best captured by one manager's response to the question, "Are you aspiring to further promotions or upward career moves within or outside of your company?" He responded with determination and enthusiasm, "Always!"

Strong Religious Orientation

Consistent with empirical indicators in the literature of the importance of religion in the lives of black Americans (see Lincoln & Mamiya, 1990), in an overriding sense, religion plays a vital role in the lives of the managers and their families. It factored in as a part of their childhood experience and continues in their adult lives in varying ways and degrees. Religious orientation was assessed on the basis of three criteria: a family history of religious involvement, rates of current church attendance, and self-assessments of religiosity.

As children, all respondents (100%) and their spouses attended church on a weekly or more frequent basis. All but a few, on a scale of responses ranging from *very often* to *never*, responded that they now attend church *sometimes* to *very often*. Only four respondents said *rarely* or *never*. In three quarters of the families, the children also attend church. In those families where parents and children attend church, most do so together as a family. The rate of church attendance was higher for managers with children than for those without children.

When asked, "Do you consider yourself to be a religious person?," all but three responded "yes." The group of non-churchgoers and those who reported themselves as being religious persons were not mutually exclusive. That is, some of those respondents who reported rare or no church attendance still considered themselves religious. Not attending church did not necessarily indicate a lack of religious belief. A possible explanation for this finding may lie in the fact that as children they were involved in the church, were brought up in the belief that religion was important, and were steeped in Christian values. Even within the group of infrequent or non-churchgoers, many indicated that Christian values influence how they live their lives and that they instilled these values in their children.

Strong Kinship Bonds

The variable of strong kinship bonds was operationalized by several items that tested for family support on varying levels. Included were questions about the frequency of verbal, written, and face-to-face communication; involvement in kin support networks and the nature of support by type of support lent; and the accessibility, frequency of use, reciprocity, source, and importance of such networks for them. Although we were most interested here in extended kinship relationships or bonds with family members residing outside of the household, we were also able to obtain important information regarding the nature of support among immediate family members, especially support between managers and their spouses.

On a 5-point scale, ranging from *very often* to *never,* most (153, $N = 191$) described their frequency of communication with family members residing outside of the household as *very often* to *often*. Some respondents, including some who described their contact as *frequent,* said that their communication was not frequent enough. All (100%) indicated communication with some degree of positive frequency, ranging from as often as *once a day* to at least *once a month*. For most (148, $N = 174$), communication was at least one time per week.

Generally, visiting patterns among kin could be described as frequent. Geographic distance, although it did not seem to affect significantly the frequency of communication, did have some impact on the frequency of visiting family members. The frequency of visiting family members ranged from a few times weekly to much less frequently depending on geographic propinquity. The closer respondents lived to relatives, the more frequently they saw them. Those who lived within 75 miles of relatives visited on an average of approximately once a month. Those who resided at a greater distance generally saw relatives less frequently. Although the type of communication (face-to-face vs. other) was somewhat affected, frequency of communication patterns was not severely altered by distance. Even those who lived far away from relatives had frequent communication with them.

Having achieved middle-class status, with six exceptions, managers do not receive financial support from their kinship networks, although most had while in college (101, $N = 155$), and some had early in their careers or when their children were younger. On the contrary, many now give or have given financial support to other family members including parents, siblings, nieces, and nephews. More than half (110, $N = 191$) also reported that at some point in the past or at present, a relative (including in-laws) resided in their household. In some cases, this involved a mother who provided child-care support. In others, it was a sibling between jobs or in the process of relocating, or a niece or nephew staying for the summer.

We found that relatives are more likely to provide managers and their families with support of a psychosocial nature. Respondents ranked emotional support as the primary type of support received (126, $N = 191$); advice (47) and child care (48) ranked second. Support on the level of child care assistance, help in problem solving, and of a spiritual nature were also frequently cited in addition to emotional support.

When asked who among their relatives provides them with understanding, advice, or support, an array of relations were cited including siblings, parents, mothers-in-law, grandparents, aunts, and uncles. Sometimes a special sibling, such as an older brother, was mentioned in this connection. The most frequently mentioned relative was one's mother (131, $N = 161$). Some listed quite a few relatives that they could turn to if needed. A few included individuals who might fall under the category of surrogate kin. Everyone (100%) indicated that there was someone among their kin on whom they could depend for understanding, advice, and support.

We also inquired as to the direction of support. All but one (190, $N = 191$) indicated that support networks were reciprocal; although, as has been stated, the nature of the support may be of a different type. Regarding accessibility or availability, support was generally exchanged whenever asked for.

Family was ranked first by all of the respondent managers except one (190, $N = 191$) as the greatest source of support above friends, church, or other. Many described their families as "close-knit." When asked the question, "How important do you consider their (family) help and support to be in your life?," responses were all very positive. Many displayed facial expressions and other body language that reinforced their statements and emphasized the high level of importance to them of family support. Their responses included the following:

"Extremely valuable. My mother has given me very good advice on so many things over the years."

"Very valuable. If I didn't have it, I don't know what I'd do."

"Even if I don't need their support, it's extremely important to me to know that I can count on their support."

"Very. Gives another point of view."

"Critically important. The black family is one of our few institutions."
"Family is an important part of my personal life."

The importance of family could also be seen in the way respondents spoke of their families of procreation, the families they formed through marriage, and the types of involvement they have with their families. A strong family orientation was shown by many managers and spouses, who said that they limit those leisure activities that do not include their children. Mothers especially make it a priority to spend a maximum amount of time with their children. Vacations are usually taken as a family and the place visited or activities engaged in are often child oriented (e.g., Disneyland).

Parents appear to be highly child oriented even in reconstituted families. Many of the fathers could be described as being very involved with their children, although most were average in this regard, and a few only fair. Of the male managers, 112 ($N = 126$) said that they spend time three to five evenings per week with their children. As a group, they engaged in activities including giving their children baths, reading stories, checking homework, putting children to bed, and transporting them to school, lessons, and other activities. Some, including several who were highly involved with their children, stated that they did not have as much involvement with them as they would like to because of their long work hours. Respondents spoke warmly and respectfully about their spouses. Unsolicited self-reports revealed a sense of pride in one's spouse.

In general, as is consistent with the literature on family support among blacks (see Jayakody, Chatters, & Taylor, 1993; Stack, 1996; Taylor, 1990; Taylor, Chatters, & Mays, 1988), all respondents valued their immediate and extended families very highly for both practical and ideological reasons, regardless of differences in circumstances or experience. As one respondent shared, "Family is important to us. We connect them (children) whenever possible. In summers, we board nieces and nephews so that kids can have contact with relatives. Family is valued even if relatives represent a different slice of life."

Support was found for all five of Robert Hill's (1971) identified black family strengths. Indeed, a high degree of support was found for all except role flexibility, which was supported but with qualification. This point requires some elaboration. I assert that role flexibility was the least supported because of the lack of reciprocity between husbands and wives. Husbands received a great deal of support from their wives and this strength and support appears to be essential to the pursuit of their careers. Husbands engaged in some nontraditional gender role behaviors; however, wives are more gender role flexible than husbands, assuming their husbands' domestic responsibilities more frequently than husbands assume those of their wives. We might conclude that once middle-class status is acquired, husbands/fathers tend to exhibit fairly traditional gender role behaviors with respect to engaging in domestic tasks.

To conclude our discussion of Hill's other strengths as they characterize black corporate families, education and hard work were found to be highly valued among the respondents. Respondents were success oriented and looked forward to continued career and personal success. Furthermore, we can surmise that parental support, especially regarding education, was important, if not necessary, for success.

Religion appears to be an important stabilizing force in the lives of black managers and their families, even for the nonchurch going respondents in the sample. Both churchgoers and non-churchgoers passed their Christian values on to their children.

Examining communication, support networks, and the importance of family, we found kinship bonds among the members of black corporate families to be tenacious. Respondents indicated directly and indirectly a close connectedness to kin. They enjoyed frequent communication with extended family members even if they were geographically distant. Most families could be described as "close-knit." Managers participated in highly active kinship networks, characterized by levels of support that were reciprocal although not in kind. They were more likely to receive support of an emotional nature whereas they often gave support of a financial nature. Although support from all family members was valued, mothers' support was most highly valued. In general, family was highly valued, and children were especially valued.

Linking Strengths to Stresses

On initial consideration, it might appear that Robert Hill's (1971) five strengths, although extremely important in black family life, only seem to strengthen and support African Americans as families in a general sense—however, they may not support them directly in all cases vis-à-vis their particular stresses. In other words, they may not be stress-specific strengths. But, more important, being a strong, well-shored-up family reinforces one's ability to cope with stress, whatever its nature or specific form.

To offer a simplistic organic example, although we may not ingest the recommended doses of vitamin C specific to warding off a cold, if in other ways we do things to maintain the physical self in a healthy manner— regular exercise, proper rest and diet—we may be armed or strengthened against the common cold.

All of the five strengths may not tie directly to the specific stresses that black corporate managers and their families face, but they certainly bolster these managers so that they are better able to cope with stress, which can include racism and all of its related problems such as race-related child-rearing issues, problems associated with relocation, marginality, and tokenism.

On the other hand, however, in an overriding way these particular strengths do affect or create the kind of individual who can deal with racism; for example, one who has

- those strengths that build self-esteem such as strong kinship bonds and a strong religious orientation;
- a strong religious orientation, including the belief that all people have the potential to be "human" and better than they are;
- adaptability of family roles as a family trait, in that you know that someone is there to help you carry your load;
- a strong achievement orientation, to be successful despite the obstacles, whatever they may be; and
- a strong work orientation, and the willingness to work hard no matter the type of work or the conditions (including adverse ones) that prevail.

From this perspective, these black family strengths are operative in the double ABCX Model (Component B; McCubbin & Patterson, 1983). Black family cultural strengths enter into the mix as resources, resources that allow one to cope with the varying and variable crises of racism (Component A). These strengths arm black families against the sources of stress that they face in corporate America.

In the next chapter, we explore black women, work, and interpersonal relations. We include a focus on a group for whom the absence of a family and children of their own challenges their sense of self and self-assessments of success: upwardly mobile single black women in corporate America.

5

Women, Work, and Interpersonal Relationships

I think being a woman means you have to work harder to prove yourself. As a black woman—it's only compounded by that fact.

—Beatrice Cunningham, black female manager

This chapter focuses on the female managers in the sample. It is divided into two sections. The first addresses the subject of work and the experience of being black and female. The second and major section of the chapter looks at interpersonal relations and the problems of mate selection. The chapter explores the historical experiences of black women and work and the issues of racism and sexism, and the importance of marriage and family, particularly for those successful black women for whom these are absent.

Black Women and Work

Although women's participation in the labor force increased during World War I and has steadily risen since World War II, women remained strangers to corporate management until the early 1970s. Women worked in corporations, of course, as clerks and secretaries, as "pink-collar" workers. The liberation movements of the late 1960s and early

1970s changed our thinking about women's social roles. The growing acceptance of women as workers, the increased opportunities for women in higher education, and affirmative action training and hiring programs created the female manager.

Affirmative action policies, those for blacks and those for women, opened corporate managerial doors to the black female. Although she was no stranger to the world of work, unlike her white counterpart, out of economic necessity and because of racial discrimination against black men (see Freeman, 1990), she was new to the higher ranks of the corporate world.

Comparing the labor force participation rates of black women versus white women as early as 1890, we find that approximately 40% of black women were employed outside of the home compared with only 16% of white women (Richardson, 1986). We know that today more than half of the women in both race groups are part of the U.S. labor force (58.8% of all women as of 1994, projected to rise to 63% by the year 2005 according to the Bureau of Labor Statistics, 1995). The world of work has been a familiar one to black women since their arrival in the United States as slaves, and although most women today, regardless of race, work out of necessity, a slightly higher percentage of black women than white are employed.

In fact, black women have a higher labor force participation rate than white, Asian, or Hispanic women. Even when marital status is controlled for, this phenomenon holds true. The labor force participation rate of married versus single black women remains higher than for married women in other groups, for example, 65.6% for black women versus 60.3% for white women in 1994 (Bureau of Labor Statistics, 1995). This is largely because black men earn less than white men, and unemployment rates for black men tend to average more than twice that of white men, for example, 12.0% versus 5.4%, respectively, in 1994 (Bureau of Labor Statistics, 1995). The black family is more dependent on women's wages, and the Bureau of Labor Statistics for 1980 and 1990 show that black women contribute a greater percentage of their family's total support than do white women. Although about half of black families today, contrary to popular belief, are dual headed, we might also note that black women more often than white tend to be heads of households (Glick, 1997). These black women are often the sole supporters of themselves and their children.

A closer look at comparisons between black female and white female employment yields some interesting and important facts. The work status of the two groups is similar because most women are concentrated in clerical, operative, and service areas of work, and are in low-paying, low-status occupations. But the profiles of the two groups begin to change as we observe that black women tend to be unemployed (and underemployed) more often than white women—11.0% versus 5.2%, respectively, unemployment in 1994 (Bureau of Labor Statistics, 1995). When we move on to compare black females who are professionals and managers with white women we find that, despite their higher labor force participation rates, black women do not fare as well. Fewer black women in the workforce are professionals (12.7% vs. 16.9%) or managers (3.0% vs. 6.7%) than are white women (Bureau of Labor Statistics, 1990). Thus, on closer examination, the on-the-surface similarities yield to inequalities. The same holds true as we move up the status ranks to the more prestigious types of employment.

DUAL MINORITY STATUS: BLACK AND FEMALE

Black women hold a unique status in the world of work. They are set apart from males because of their sex but they are also distinctive among women because of race. Although we know that individually the statuses of race and sex serve as stratifiers in labor force participation, there is a divergence of views pertaining to the significance of the two factors in combination.

There are two predominant but opposing views of black women's position in the labor force. In the first view, black women are subject to the double, even triple, "whammy" of prejudice and discrimination on the basis of sex, race, and class as well. We might also consider the possible interactive effects of Race × Sex, Race × Class, Sex × Class, and Race × Sex × Class. Because of these status identities, according to this view black women are clearly the objects of a threefold disadvantage. According to the second view, black women are seen as having the advantage of race over white women. Epstein (1973), a proponent of this view, states that the two negatives of sex and race create a positive. Black women are less often perceived as sex role stereotypes. They are not seen as being in the business world to find a husband, nor seen as likely to drop out because of getting married, or requiring "delicate" treatment because of their femininity. In short, they are not perceived as women.

Therefore, the identity of being black works to cancel out the identity of being female so that black women are less likely to be subject to sexism in the workplace.

Although they may not be perceived according to the same sex role stereotypes as are white women (there is another set of sex role stereotypes that are applied to black women), there is little evidence to support this second view that black women benefit from their double oppression overall. When looking at sex role stereotypes about women and work, black women are still concentrated in the female-dominated professions such as teaching, social work, and nursing, respectively. Looking at overall earnings, black women rank fourth, earning less than white women, black men, and white men, respectively. Although black women may earn as much or slightly more than white women in some professional and managerial jobs, there are plausible explanations that preclude their race status as being an advantage. Specifically, because employment for black men since slavery has always been tenuous, there has always been a greater need for black women versus white women to participate in the paid labor force to support themselves and their families. Because black women have a longer history in the work world, and are less likely to interrupt their careers because of marriage or child rearing, they are likely to have a longer rate of tenure and be paid more because of longevity in the job. (Some of the women interviewed in the sample argue that they are also often better educated than white women in the same job.) This does not necessarily mean higher-status jobs, but rather higher pay in the same job because of tenure. Still, a smaller percentage of black women are employed as managers and professionals than are white women. Furthermore, Bailey, Wolfe, and Wolfe (1996) suggest that black women compared with white women (and men) are less likely to receive adequate and appropriate social support in the diverse work environment of today.

To further support the notion that black women suffer oppression and discrimination on the basis of sex, we would find it fruitful to compare them with black men. Although more black women are professionals (e.g., teachers) than black men, black men have steadily expanded their presence in the professions and in management since World War II and enjoy a wider representation in a greater variety of professions. Black men also enjoy higher status, higher prestige, and higher-paying professional jobs. To compare black men and women in the labor force in management and administration, we find approximately 6% males to approximately 4% females (Bureau of Labor Statistics, 1990). Many of these jobs, especially those in corporate America, are higher status, higher paying than the traditional female professional jobs, and specifically for blacks within the corporate ranks, males tend to have higher-status jobs than females.

We can conclude that being black and female in the workplace holds no advantage for black women in status and money over white women or black men. Racism and sexism both affect negatively black women's status in the labor market. But the effects of the two stratifiers and discriminators are not clear-cut.

WHAT THIS STUDY REVEALS: RACE OR SEX?

A question often raised in professional and personal circles about racism and sexism is, "Which is greater?" Are black women more disadvantaged because of their race or their sex? To further complicate an answer to this question, the fact is that it is sometimes hard to tell whether one is facing racial discrimination or gender discrimination. Many of the women employed in the corporate environment that I spoke with experienced this confusion. Black female managers were sometimes uncertain whether the type of response they received from peers and superiors was due to their identity as black, or female, or the combination of the two. Questions and ambiguities such as these are consistent with Fox and Hesse-Biber's (1984) conclusion: "Thus the situation for black women, including black professional women, appears to be more complex and more negative than the image provided by popular myths and stereotypes" (p. 173).

Many of those who hold that having dual minority status (black and female) was more of a negative than having only one or the other status have assumed that these statuses are cumulative. That is, having both statuses is twice as bad as having one. I would like to suggest that these statuses may not be cumulative. In fact, it is more likely that they are interactive. It seems apparent that further research is needed on this subject to inform us of the similarities of experience between black women and black men (effects by race), and between black women and white women (effects by sex), as well as the differences, and the combined interactive effects of both race and sex (see Smith & Stewart, 1983, for a further preliminary discussion of this notion).

The female managers in this study were asked to give subjective appraisals of their experience with racism and sexism. When asked,

"Which has been the greater source of discrimination for you: racism or sexism?," the response was overwhelmingly "racism." When asked, "Would you say this is true for most black women?," the response was (almost) unanimously affirmative.

Beatrice Cunningham, a black female manager interviewed for this study, in her own voice, shares the views and sentiments expressed by many of the black female respondents on issues of racism and sexism:

Question: What problems do you as a black female corporate manager have that other managers do not have?

I think being a woman means you have to work harder to prove yourself. As a black woman, it's only compounded by that fact. So, I do find that I have a certain standard of performance and it means putting unnecessary pressure and stress on myself because I want to excel. I don't want to make mistakes. Everybody makes mistakes, but you feel a lot more vulnerable when you do versus someone else. I think that you do have to work harder than your white male counterparts.

Question: Does sexism exist in your company?

Yes, although it's not always blatant, but one would have to be incredibly naive to say that it didn't.

Question: Which is the greater problem: racism or sexism?

Racism (emphatic response). I don't feel that there is the commitment or the interest in promoting minorities in my company or in most others. We tend to get to middle management, some a little above that, and that's generally where we plateau. We have no black general managers in this corporation and we have no black officers in the company and we do have one woman.

Question: Do you feel you have an advantage over white women in the workplace because you are both female and black?

No (emphatic response).

Thus, black women managers in the corporation, based on this research, feel that in their own lives as well as for other black female managers, racism versus sexism is a more pervasive problem and that racism is the greater source of discrimination. This view concurs with other scholarly findings including that of Rodgers-Rose's (1980) assessment, in her treatise on the black woman, that race differences are greater than sex differences in affecting black women's discrimination. Although we must concede that there is not much research on black females in management, we can conclude on the basis of the findings of this study (consistent with those of others) that black women in the corporate workplace are disadvantaged by both race and sex, and the greater disadvantage is incurred by race.

Problems in Interpersonal Relationships for Black Professional Women

THE ROLE OF EDUCATION

Although it has not been unusual historically for black women to be more educated than black men, a higher level of education now provides a different level of opportunity for educated blacks and a more affluent lifestyle with its associated tastes, preferences, and alternative values.

Male-female educational gaps have grown, while, at the same time, the new significance or meaning of this gap has come to separate the life courses of less educated black men and more highly educated black women. Education, in this respect, in recent years, has had a divergent effect on black lifestyles and has a negative impact on black male-female interpersonal relationships. Specifically, it poses problems for the disproportionately high number of black singles, and especially for the disproportionately high number of well-educated black women within this group, such as the black female corporate manager, in mate selection.

Education is now more closely linked to job status for black women (as well as men) in new and diverse ways. The significance of education for blacks, especially women, has changed, now creating greater options for jobs and lifestyles. It now not only serves to protect black women from indignities—the drudgery and degradation of domestic employ and the possibility of sexual abuse—but allows her, to a certain degree, to integrate into the mainstream culture.

Integration in education and employment were among the black community's goals in the 1950s and 1960s. Although with significant limitations, these goals have been achieved. In their struggles for equal opportunity, black activists of 30 and 40 years ago could not have conceived of the fact that achieving these goals and thus finding solutions to race problems could pose new ones.

The Decision to Educate Daughters

Despite the bias in U.S. culture in the direction of the male sex, blacks have had their own subcultural dictums and modes of adaptation to living in a white-dominated society that shape their values and behaviors. In several respects, black families have historically shown favor toward educating black women. That is, regarding education, families who were able to send perhaps only one of their offspring to college often chose to educate their daughters. This was done to spare their female children from a life of drudgery and the degradation of domestic work as a maid or washerwoman, and the possibility of sexual abuse that they might be subjected to in domestic employ. Their sons would have to fend for themselves. The thinking was that if their daughters did not marry, they could support themselves as schoolteachers versus as maids. Where families could afford only a year or two of college, parents hoped that in that length of time their daughters could find husbands who would provide for them, again sparing them the indignity and vulnerability of employment as a domestic. Providing for the education of daughters rather than sons was an attempt by fathers (and mothers) to protect their daughters and their future well-being. For black women, it could be argued that education was seen not so much as a route to economic opportunity via gaining high wage-earning employment, but rather as a way for them to avoid domestic employ and indignities resulting from white racism, as well as to get "well married." It was a route to a life of dignity and one in which her virtue would be protected.

The Changing Functions and
Dysfunctions of Higher Education

As times have changed and as the doors to a wider range of jobs have opened to blacks and to women, the function of education for black women has broadened. Blacks in the past who were college educated became lawyers, doctors, clergymen, teachers, and nurses. For women, for the most part, only the latter two were options for them among the professions. Those who did become teachers or nurses practiced their professions within the confines of black schools and black hospitals. For example, Dunbar High School in Washington, D.C., a school for blacks during segregation, at one point in its history had a teaching faculty consisting of 68% Ph.D.s—there were no other job opportunities for educated blacks. Although job opportunities today remain limited, they have expanded in terms of the career spheres now open to blacks. There are now other high-status alternatives to the previously named professions.

Although there have been college-educated blacks in the United States since the 1830s and an educated black middle-class population of some size for many years, the impact of education on relationships between and among blacks has changed. Because of desegregation, differences in educational achievement between males and females pose problems in male-female relationships. By opening doors once closed to blacks, such as those of the corporation, blacks with a higher level of educational achievement can enter these and other doors, leaving the bulk of blacks behind. For some blacks, the corporation functions not only as an avenue for upward mobility regarding economic advancement, but also serves as a gateway to further cultural assimilation into the mainstream. By providing opportunity to some on the basis of educational attainment, the gap is widened between those who have achieved and those who have not. Cultural contact in the work environment with mainstream culture has the effect of fostering greater assimilation into the main-stream when it comes to values, tastes, and lifestyles. Black women, successful in the corporation, begin to find themselves increasingly dis-tanced from the bulk of blacks and the bulk of single black men. As Dorothy Height, president of the National Council of Negro Women aptly puts it, "Because racism historically conferred the same status on all blacks, regardless of education or profession, women of past genera-tions were less likely to let job status obstruct a relationship" ("Dorothy Height on Racism," 1986).

Today, status achievement and the accompanying sociocultural vari-ations yield greater status differentials within the black community, which function as barriers in the mate selection process.

OBSTACLES AND OPTIONS IN MATE SELECTION

In their search for mates, black women have been charged with being too materialistic; too demanding in their mate selection criteria, only considering the titled, high-salaried black male; and not exploring their other options, such as romantic liaisons with blue-collar men, men of other ethnic backgrounds, and even man sharing. Even experts (Staples, 1981) and civic and community leaders have suggested that these options may provide the only avenues for romance for a significant number of black professional women.

Black women in the dating game are buyers in a seller's market. According to Staples (1981), the single black female cannot be too demanding of black men because these men can go elsewhere. The educated, well-employed single black male is a scarce commodity, and he, therefore, can pick and choose among black women. But most black women are not willing to settle for less than their ideal. They will not compromise their values, "just to have a man."

A partial explanation for black professional women's tenacity in their search for an ideal mate can be offered on the basis of the findings of studies on the mate selection process (Robinson, 1995; Staples, 1981), and my interviews with black female managers as well.

Black women, like white women, have been influenced by the romantic dream of waiting for their knight in shining armor, their own "Prince Charming" (see Robinson, 1995). They are also women who have been reared to believe that because of their own educational backgrounds and career achievements, they are deserving of mates with stature and earning power equal to theirs. Furthermore, theories of mate selection that view the courtship process as a system of exchange support this notion. That is, the more positive qualities one has to offer to a prospective mate, the more positive qualities one can expect to get in return. A woman who, in her view, has an abundance of highly desirable qualities might reasonably expect to attract a mate who also has an abundance of desirable qualities.

Professional black women who are educated and employed in the corporate managerial ranks are likely to have acquired, through their life experiences, some tastes and interests that are reflective of those experiences. That is, they are more likely to be assimilated into the mainstream and are likely to have acquired some of the cultural trappings of that group. Black men who have not had similar experiences are not likely to have the same interests, likes, and dislikes. Furthermore, Bailey et al. (1996) suggest that black women employed in racially diverse settings (such as in corporate America) are less likely to receive adequate personal social support from spouses if these spouses have no experience with similar work environments, and therefore these spouses may lack the necessary "knowing empathy" to be supportive. The findings of mate selection research contradict the old saying that opposites attract. Rather, attitude similarity is one of the greatest factors influencing the mate selection process (Centers, 1975; Stephens, 1985). Black female managers are not unlike others who want a mate whose lifestyle and interests affirm and reinforce their own. The black woman who enjoys tennis, escargot, and Rachmaninoff will be more likely to find a mate who shares similar interests in the ranks of the (upper) middle class rather than the working class.

WHY THE BIG DEAL ABOUT MATE SELECTION?

Given the high levels of career success of many black professional women, which were achieved against the odds, why then is finding a mate so important? Why isn't occupational success enough? The answers to these questions rest in the context of the influence of cultural values. We tend to think of family as being a necessary and universally desired aspect of human adult life. Family has been said to be the supreme goal of adult life. This is said to be especially true for women. The socialization process and societal bias prepare and push women, in particular, in the direction of establishing traditional family lives. Although it is somewhat true for both sexes that individuals in our culture are made to feel self-conscious about their marital status, it is especially true in the case of women. Blacks are not immune to dominant cultural sex role prescriptions. Furthermore, emphasis on the importance of family is a dominant characteristic of black culture as well. As was noted in Chapters 2 and 4, a strong kinship orientation is one of the five traditional black family strengths identified by Robert Hill (1971). The black family has often been looked on as the single most important factor contributing historically to the survival of blacks in the United States.

Black managerial and professional women are no exception to the gender-specific norms for women in general and for black women in particular. Pouring one's energies into preparing for and working hard to build a high-powered career does not mean that marriage and family are not important to them. Nor are they any less important than they are to other women who have not achieved such professional heights. Upwardly mobile successful women do not necessarily choose career over family. Because the family role of wife and mother is so highly valued and normatively proscribed for women in American and African

American cultures, even the most occupationally successful black women are likely to devalue their overall personal success if they do not have a mate—in spite of having achieved exceptional heights in other areas of their lives. Striving to find a mate, despite professional accomplishments, is likely to remain pivotal in the life quests of single black female managers, even to the point of overshadowing their other accomplishments and future occupational goals.

POSTPONING MARRIAGE FOR CAREER

The current literature on marriage patterns asserts that it is necessary for both males and females to postpone marriage to pursue the higher levels of education now required for today's job market. This is offered as an explanation for demographers' statistics regarding the trend from the 1950s toward later marriage in the 1990s. This pattern is most strongly observable among the middle class, who are more likely to go to college, and for those aspiring to a career versus a job.

Women have entered the job market in greater and greater numbers since World War II, but especially since the 1960s. (Again, of course, black women, including some middle-class women, have traditionally worked outside of the home.) In the early 1970s, the number of women in the workforce with children under 18 years of age increased and reached what Bernard (1975a, 1975b) calls the "tipping point" (e.g., when the normative pattern of the past becomes the option exercised by the minority), when more than half of U.S. women were employed outside of the home. Whereas the phenomenon of the majority of women, including those with preschool-age children, working in the paid labor force is a relatively new one (only about 30 years old), postponement of marriage and family in the interest of education and work is a more revolutionary phenomenon for females than for males. (Males in the middle class and males aspiring to the professions have traditionally delayed marriage.)

The price to be paid for career success, however, lies in the realm of interpersonal relationships. Today's mate selection pool is imbalanced. USA Today ("Dorothy Height on Racism," 1986) reported that there are approximately 1.5 million more black adult women than black men in the United States (25% more women) according to 1984 census projections. The imbalance among whites is 10% more women than men. Black sociologist Robert Staples (1981) tells us that the situation is even more critical for black women not just in numbers but in eligibility and the characteristics of those in the mate selection pool (e.g., differences in education and socioeconomic factors, cultural preferences, values, and so on). Staples says that most eligible (not on drugs or incarcerated) single black men are less well educated than the eligible pool of single black women, and are more likely to be nonprofessionals. The higher up the ladder of education and career success a black woman climbs, the greater are her chances of remaining single.

Current research findings (see Zinn & Eitzen, 1987) inform us that women over the age of 30, 35, and 40 progressively have a lessening chance at marriage. Once again, the statistics are significantly more pessimistic for black women. For many women, especially black women, the result of postponing marriage in the interest of pursuing education and building career may be never marrying at all.

WHAT SINGLE FEMALE RESPONDENTS HAD TO SAY

The women I interviewed indicated that their ideal mate would be a black man. They felt that they shared more in common with black men versus white, and said that they were more physically attracted to black versus other types of men. Although several of the women indicated that they had dated men of other races, their preferences for marriage were black men. It appears, then, that the notion of similars attracting carries over to racial similarity as well. This preference is consistent with marriage statistics by race, which inform us that Americans are homogamous in their mate selection practices (see Adams, 1995, pp. 238-239 for statistics on black-white intermarriage). They tend to marry within their own group on the basis of race and other factors as well. The continuing low incidence of interracial marriage attests to this.

In romance as in other areas, black middle-class women tend to be fairly traditional and conservative in their values. Although some women attested to having dated married men, or having been in relationships with men who were admittedly not monogamous, the "one woman, one man" arrangement was valued by most of the women that I interviewed as the arrangement of preference. One woman said, "I'm not into sharing. I want my own man or I can do without!" The traditional U.S. family ideal, black and white, of man, woman, and their children, or the monogamous pattern of family, is valued and upheld by the black managerial women in the sample.

Although it might be foolish not to admit the possibility of a certain degree of snobbism, class consciousness, or materialism on the part of some middle-class black women, we must also give credence to the validity of the aforementioned explanations of why more black managerial women do not pursue what some have posed to be viable options for romance. They feel that they are deserving of a high-status mate. They seek mates with whom they share similar interests and experiences, and they value highly the institution of monogamous marriage. One woman that I interviewed said,

> I want a man with whom I can share my ideas and interests. I'm open to dating different kinds of men but when it comes to marriage I want someone who'll be an equal partner who I can have a relationship that fulfills all of my needs. Otherwise, I'll stay on my own and keep looking, and if I find the right man, fine.
>
> —Sonia Roberts, age 33

Of the managers I interviewed, only 36% of the women were married. These women have not chosen career instead of marriage as a permanent alternative. Rather, they uphold traditional values that affirm that marriage and family are important in one's life. Therefore, the fact that they are single is likely to reflect the reality of a limited available selection pool and not of an alternative set of values that does not hold marriage in high esteem.

My interviewees, in detailing their personal experiences, shed some light on the complexities of being black, female, professional, and single. Lynn Jeffries's profile, in many respects, exemplifies those of most other female respondents of her marital and professional status along several of the dimensions discussed in this chapter (e.g., she is highly successful yet that success is tempered by the lack of a mate; her preferences in, experiences with, and obstacles to mate selection) in a particularly poignant fashion.

PROFILE: LYNN JEFFRIES

Lynn Jeffries is a 38-year-old female manager at the office of the national headquarters of her corporation. She has been with the corporation for 9 years. Although this is not her first job after college (she worked as a state employee immediately after completing undergraduate school), it is her first corporate job. She is single (never married) and has no children.

Lynn has enjoyed a good degree of mobility up the corporate ladder. In the 9 years that she's been with her company, she has been promoted four times. Her salary has grown commensurate with her promotions. She earns about $75,000 per year.

From a lower-middle-class background, Lynn has experienced greater career achievement than her female siblings and has done about as well as her older brother. She has also outperformed most of her childhood peers in the realm of career. She attributes her greater success compared with others in her hometown to personal ability and drive, different value systems, and parental encouragement in her studies, especially from her mother. Always a good student, she graduated college making the Dean's List.

Lynn has dated a wide variety of types of men—some white, some black; most although not all professional men; and one who was married. As an adult, she has had two long-term relationships with men. Her preference for dating and for marriage is black men. At present, she is not involved in a steady relationship.

By all outward appearances, we would consider Lynn Jeffries to be a successful black woman. She is well educated, well salaried, and well employed, enjoying a comfortable lifestyle. But when the question, "Do you consider yourself to be successful?," was asked, the response Lynn gave, after a long pause, was a mixed one.

Although Lynn has achieved on all of the above criteria, she clearly makes a distinction between professional and personal achievement. She is proud of her achievements in business and talks of them with confidence and ease. Yet, she remains unfulfilled. Aware of the benefits and rewards of life in corporate management, Lynn is also aware of the costs to her happiness and contentment in her personal life. The price is paid by the limitations her work situation puts on her ability to build friendships with other blacks who might share her interests and capabilities. But especially significant for Lynn, who would like to marry, is that her ability to establish and maintain a satisfying intimate relationship with a man has been impeded. This "successful," accomplished young woman, whose high salary affords her many of life's comforts, admits to sometimes feeling lonely.

A part of her feels that she should be satisfied with all that she does have and with what she has achieved. At the same time, she also has moments of self-denigration when she wonders if she is doing something wrong or if there is something about her that causes her to attract the wrong kinds of men. Lynn remains optimistic that marriage is still a possibility for her in the future, when the right man comes along. Meanwhile, she misses what she refers to as a sense of "balance" in her life, attained from having both career and family. She is very much aware, as are many of the managers that I have talked to, that family serves a very important function as a leveling factor in one's life, keeping the stresses and glories of life in the corporate world in perspective.

Question: Do you consider yourself to be successful?

Um . . . yes . . . I guess so. Personally, I have a different view of what success means, but professionally I've been successful in that I am the first black female manager in the corporate headquarters, I was the first black professional employee to be promoted, and the last promotion I got was as a result of the chairman of the board. I think I'm paid well for what I do. I think about, at one time I said, "Gee, if I ever make $20,000 per year I don't know what I would do." And it wasn't that long ago that I said that, and since I moved here from where I was when I was promoted, I've tripled my salary. So, I guess from that point of view, I feel that I've done some things that, or, things that have happened have been positive. (She takes a deep breath.)

As for the personal side . . . well it's kind of like after you've accomplished certain things you say, "Well, okay, now that you've done this, now what?" You have some type of professional recognition, your career seems to be taking off rather well but there are a lot of trade-offs that you make. And one, being here in (name of suburban town), I feel very isolated. Because of the type of community that I live in, I don't feel that there are other black professional peers for me to meet as a single person. So, I have felt lonely and isolated, and in some of my personal relationships with men, for different reasons, perhaps because of my success and their careers maybe not taking off like mine, it's caused other kinds of problems. So, I think I would say, okay, you make a fairly good salary and there're things that you can do that financial resources will allow you to do, but then there's the other part of your life where you say what good is it to have this if you don't have somebody else in your life, you know, to appreciate this. And, I guess I just haven't found that yet. I guess maybe I'm being too hard on myself when I'm saying that I haven't been as successful in that area of my life as I have been professionally.

Question: How would you describe your dating patterns?

I have dated both black men and white men. There were times when, if I wanted to go out at all, I had to date white men because that was all that was really available. I had one long-term relationship with a black man that ended shortly after I came here. (Lynn relocated to a town 40 miles away when she received a promotion to corporate headquarters a few years ago.) And, I think that had a lot to do directly with the promotion that I got because he could not handle the fact that I was going to be making twice as much money as he was, along with other problems that we had, but that was sort of the straw that broke the camel's back.

Question: What do you see as the biggest obstacle to your having a steady relationship with a man?

I'm not really sure that I can answer that. The reason I say that is that part of what I've been doing for the last year and a half is that I have been involved in counseling, and one of the things that we talk about is me in relationships with people, and I'm not sure if it's partly my fault or if it's just timing, or, that what I view that I need or want in a mate I've just not met, so I can't really answer that. I'd like to say I've not really been in a situation where there has been a variety of different kinds of people, you know, where I can say, gee, I like him. I'd like to go out with him. I don't feel that I have a problem attracting men. I've just gotten over that hurdle though 6 months ago with my doctor. 'Cause when I stop and think about the different people I've been involved with, that's not the case. And I think another thing that I should mention is that I've been involved with a married man. It met a personal need, and was satisfying enough, we saw each other enough and did things. It didn't require any commitment. But I found that was not what I wanted at all, and that I was selling myself short, so I subsequently ended the relationship, but that went on for a couple of years.

Question: What is the most difficult thing for you to find in your relationships with men?

I think emotional support. I think that that is one of the things that I feel is important and I haven't found that in many of the people that I've been involved with. I don't know what the reasons are. I want someone who can be supportive of me and what I want to do regarding my career goals and also be supportive of that person and whatever they want to do, and I find that the men that I have been involved with, for the most part, don't tend to really view that as being important. It's not anything that's really discussed, it's just not there. It's like, "What do you have to complain about? You make X amount of money, you have this. What do you need that for?" And, money is not that important other than how you use that to measure whether you think you are successful or not relative to the rest of the world. So, I guess anyone who makes a certain amount of money, you say, gee, that person has done well. I would like to think that how I make my money in the career I'm in is one thing, but that is not more important than having the kind of support system that you need at home, 'cause in this kind of job it's a very stressful kind of job, and there are some times when I leave here and I say to myself, "Is it worth it?" And, if I had the type of mate I feel that I need or that I would want, then the job does not become so all consuming. It's not that important because there are other things that you have to fill your life and it provides a balance, I think.

Question: Do you ever feel different from your friends because you are part of corporate America?

Yes, some of them. I came from a very small town, and I suppose in the town that I came from I'm kind of viewed as a success story. People tend to view you as being different and kind of special, and that's positive, and that makes you feel really good. And, your friends sometimes envy you, not because they're jealous, but it just seems like, gee, that seems like a great life, you have this important job, and you know, all the things that go with a world that many people just haven't been exposed to, and you're lucky. I've ridden in limousines, and I've been exposed to a lot of different things that I perhaps would not normally have been had I not been in this kind of position, but I personally don't feel different. I just think . . . you know, my best friend is a paralegal. She was a schoolteacher for many years up until a career change about a year ago, and I don't see that as our having any problem relating to one another. We just have different experiences. But she thinks that my life is wonderful and I think hers is because she has a family and four children. I don't know. It's just really funny. I guess just differences and that's the only way that I feel different is that we have different experiences. But I don't think it makes me better or special, but I guess my friends feel that way.

My brother is in the corporate world, so I guess we talk the same language, so to speak. I have sisters who do all right in their careers, but their experiences have been different. And I think from the standpoint of having more resources financially, than they do, that they kind of think, "Gee, that's great." But they also know that . . . I don't say that I would trade it in but I would be content to be where I am, at this level in the company, if there were a person that I met that was going to provide some other things for me and I got married. I could be satisfied at this level because, who wants to make all this money and not have anybody in your life to share it with. That's really how I feel.

Lynn Jeffries, in light of her achievements, is an inspiration to younger up-and-coming black women in the corporate ranks. She is bright, personable, physically attractive, and energetic. Frequently, she engages (consciously) in formal role modeling activities. At the same time, it is sad to recognize the high price that women like Jeffries have to pay for a modicum of success in the corporate world. For many of these women, having success in career and a fulfilling personal life means making a choice between the two. It's an "either-or" proposition. Alternatively, men, as a matter of course, enjoy both.

Conclusion

Black women are not new to the workforce but are relatively new to the world of corporate management. Although they have made significant strides, there is a long way to go, and few have reached the levels that black men have reached. Unlike their black male or white female counterparts, they struggle ahead with the burden of dual minority status, being both black and female. Whereas they face discrimination from two directions, and often the nature of the discrimination is unclear (racism or sexism), they are quite definite about the fact that race rather than sex is the greater obstacle to their further achievement and upward mobility in their respective corporations.

Those women who have achieved have also paid a price for their success in interpersonal relationships. Highly educated, successful, single black women have priced themselves out of the mate selection market because the pool of eligible black males is small and typically composed of males who are less educated and have lower-status jobs. Because of the high value placed on marriage and family in society in general, and especially in the black community, these women feel something is missing in their, what some would call, almost perfect lives. They pay a high price in personal happiness for success in the job. They lack the family supports offered by marriage and children, enjoyed by most of their male counterparts on the job, which serve to cushion the stress of the corporate work environment and, at the same time, round out or "balance" their lives.

"Movers and shakers" are the focus of the next chapter. We turn our attention to black corporate families and the relocation experience.

6

Relocation

Families on the Move

I am so tired of people ringing my doorbell and asking me if the lady of the house is in.

—Geneva Hardaway, middle-aged corporate wife

At the beginning of this century, it was quite usual for a young couple to meet, marry, raise their children, and die all within the same city or town. Today, with modern technology and the demands of business and industry, this is much less likely to be the experience of many Americans. According to Blumer (1969, 1982), the structural requirements and characteristics of industrialization include the high physical mobility of workers who are motivated to be mobile to gain the best economic opportunity. Those involved in corporate employ are all too familiar with relocating because the corporation requires their services elsewhere.

Managers at IBM and Procter and Gamble have been known to refer to their organizations as "I've Been Moved" and "Pack and Go," respectively (Fernandez, 1981). Other corporate managers realize that mobility must be assumed. In the post-World War II period, as corporations grew and flourished, relocation was considered part of corporate expectations for the young upwardly mobile executive. But those times were very different. In the past few decades, the U.S. family has undergone a multiplicity of changes affecting its structure, roles, and interactive patterns. Relocation, because of job demands and in the face of these changes, has become a much more complex affair.

Today, the phenomenon of dual-career households is increasing in incidence. The rise of professionalism among women has uplifted the status of women's work outside of the home. The ever-increasing need for women to work for "bread and butter" items has resulted in increasing numbers of women being gainfully employed. Although men's work is still perceived to be more valuable in this society, expressed by the higher wages that they receive and in other ways, women's work is gaining increasing importance and is one important factor that makes relocation decisions more complicated than in the past.

Relocation can be a stressful experience for any family; it poses special problems for blacks. The result is often that families are sent to areas isolated from other blacks and where they are likely to experience racism. Relocation frequently involves uprooting blacks from cultural supports and functionally supportive kinship networks.

This chapter focuses on the relocation experience for corporate black managers and their families, their special problems, concerns, and their potential sources of support.

Research on Relocation

Fernandez (1981) is notable among researchers who have looked at the contemporary problems of corporate family relocation. In his study of managers in the Bell Telephone Company, he found that managers can expect up to 15 moves over the course of their careers. Upper-level managers were more likely to take on new assignments that required a relocation and relocated more frequently than lower-level managers— 72% of upper-level managers versus 6% of first-level managers have moved four or more times. Less educated managers were less willing to relocate even when a promotion was involved than more highly educated managers, although more highly educated managers were more concerned about where and when they would be relocated. Managers with children seemed at least as willing or more so to relocate for a promotion than managers without children. Managers believed that turning down relocations has a negative effect on one's career, especially with regard to promotions.

Women were more likely to have never relocated than men—74.1% of black women versus 61.7% of black men and 62.3% of white women versus 35.7% of white men in the sample have never relocated (Fernandez, 1981). Female managers were twice as likely to meet resistance to relocation from their spouses than were male managers. The female minority managers said that their husbands' jobs came first and theirs second when considering either partner's relocation possibilities.

Black and other minority managers were especially concerned about what part of the country and the size of the community they might be relocated to. They were less likely to accept relocations to areas where there would be few or no members of their race, or to areas that were especially known for racist treatment of minorities (Fernandez, 1981).

Fernandez (1981) concluded that to move up the corporate ladder, one must be willing to relocate several times over the course of one's career, and this was the perception held by the managers that he surveyed. The more children a manager has, the greater the need for money and, therefore, the more likely they are to relocate for a promotion— family is an incentive to earn more and to strive for career success. The husband's career still takes priority over the wife's as evidenced by female deference to husband's career when considering relocation. Those with previous relocation experience are less reluctant to relocate. Relocation has a serious emotional impact on the families of corporate managers. Finally, in response to the changing faces of corporate management, Fernandez asserts that, "the company has to become more sensitive to the very complex relocation problems that are occurring because of the changing makeup of the workforce" (p. 154).

The research efforts of others have focused on a full array of problems encountered by individuals and families in relocating to a new place. Gaylord (1984), Seidenberg (1973), and Vandervelde (1979) have focused on the problems of loss of self-esteem, lack of belonging in the community, and reacclimation to the new environment for the corporate wife. Gaylord's findings showed that corporate wives experience a loss of "traditional community supports." Often it is very difficult to become entrenched in the new community. That part of the wife's identity having to do with community status and belonging is not transferable. Gaylord also looked at the varying levels of difficulty of individual family members (e.g., a husband, a wife, a child) in adjusting to relocation. She found that women pay the greatest price for the move, then children. Most women suffer some loss, and full-time housewives especially suffer. Husbands have the least trouble adjusting to relocation.

Others have focused on the impact that moving has on children, considering their need for stability and peer support at various stages of the human development process, or the problems associated with transferring both academic and extracurricular credentials at certain critical points in their educational careers (Feldman & Elliott, 1990; Fernandez, 1981; Margolis, 1979; Seifert & Hoffnung, 1997). A few researchers (see Gershenfeld, 1986) have looked at the problems of isolation from family, friends, and community that blacks have suffered as the result of upward mobility and having to relocate to a new geographic area. But the full range of investigation into the nature of corporate relocation and its special problems for blacks and corporate relocation has not been previously reported.

Special Problems of Relocation for Blacks

Moving to a new location is a stressful event for all individuals and all families. Dohrenwend and Dohrenwend (1974) rate it high among their list of stressful life events. Warshaw (1979), in the context of discussing change of any significant nature as a stressor, focuses on corporate relocation.

On beginning my interviews with corporate managers and their families, I wondered if there might not be some operative factors that would in some ways ease the relocation experience for blacks. Respondents, however, repeatedly told me how much more difficult relocation was for blacks. They felt that racism, expressed as de facto segregation in schools, the enforcement of restricted covenants (on or off of the books) excluding blacks in housing, and the notion that community conscience is less liberal in small cities and towns where some corporations have their facilities versus large metropolitan areas were all sources of concern for managers and their families. These perceptions were based on their actual prior experiences and those of their friends, as well as the perceptions of others about whom they had heard, and from what they had read.

In general, there seem to be two factors contributing to problems in relocation for blacks: (a) a high degree of social isolation, and (b) physical distancing from kin support networks. Each of these is multifaceted in the variety of ways in which they present problems and the varying significance of the problems they cause.

Let us first consider problems of social isolation. Often relocation means moving to small towns and communities where blacks are a numerical minority. In such instances, singles have a difficult time finding eligible blacks to date. This situation is especially problematic for female managers because they are more likely to be single than male managers (see Chapter 5, this volume).

Black couples as well as singles may have only a small pool of others with whom they share similar backgrounds and black cultural experiences for establishing new friendships in these more remote areas. Social isolation for their children will mean growing up in neighborhoods where they may be the only blacks, and, therefore, they will not grow up having the benefit of black friends. The schools they attend may lack the same opportunities for peer identification with other blacks, which could help foster in them a positive sense of identity and self-worth (see Chapter 8, this volume).

Black individuals and families who live in communities where blacks are in the statistical minority will not find their (black) cultural interests and identity represented to any great extent, if at all, in community social and cultural activities such as museum exhibits, theater, celebrations, and so on. Social isolation equates with cultural deprivation for blacks. Some of the experts (Hopson & Hopson, 1990) would argue that this would create a critical deficiency in the child development experience of black children. For adult blacks, it denies them easy access to "fueling up" experiences with which to bolster themselves against the stresses of corporate America.

Isolation in the corporation as one of only a few blacks makes it more difficult to establish new social relationships with coworkers. Furthermore, the higher up in management one (black) moves, the greater the isolation, and thus the problem intensifies with increased upward mobility. Here blacks are clearly at a disadvantage compared with whites who have many others of their race with whom to form social bonds. Work is more likely to function as a source of friendships for white managers. White managers interviewed by Fernandez (1981) scored work higher in how they make new friends (whites usually ranked it first as a main source of friends compared with blacks who, in almost all cases, ranked work second and even third); 87% of whites versus 5% of blacks scored work number one as their main source of friends. In turn, white managers might be less likely to be frequently involved in and rely on extensive extended kinship networks for emotional support and social interaction.

The second factor, physical distancing from kinship networks, serves as an impediment to the functioning of the traditional black family structure and system of support. Although family is highly valued within U.S. culture, the family in African American culture has been touted as one of the important mechanisms contributing to the survival of African Americans throughout history (Toliver, 1982). Moving farther away from relatives makes it more difficult to maintain family ties. This is not to say that these networks of support become nonfunctional or that family ties become weak—they do not. Studies by McAdoo (1978) have shown the continued functioning, strength, and importance of extended family support networks for blacks in the middle class, who are likely to experience some degree of mobility. Rather, the highly mobile corporate lifestyle, in some cases, deprives individuals and families of functional daily support such as child care and frequent personal contact (e.g., sharing a meal, visiting with grandchildren and watching them grow, or joining together in some household project) that they could otherwise enjoy. Although it does not make it impossible, it certainly makes it more difficult to participate in and to avail oneself of all of the positive supports offered through the extended kinship network.

Gershenfeld (1986), in her search for an explanation for the high divorce rate among middle-class black couples, discovered that distancing from supportive kin networks as a result of increased mobility was a major factor at the root of the problem. Using a Lewinian-based theoretical framework, Gershenfeld has developed a program of intervention for assisting black middle-class families. Underlying the program is her thesis that alternative networks of supports for black families must be developed to strengthen these families as they become distanced from extended family and traditional neighborhood support systems. Gershenfeld concedes that although her program, NETWORK, which provides for the formation of a new supportive group for couples, is successful, it is not an ideal substitute for a cohesive family network of support. The type of support found within the extended family network with respect to the existence of affectional bonds, psychological and emotional support, and the durability of commitment is difficult to duplicate outside of the family context.

Findings

SUPPORTS IN THE RELOCATION PROCESS

Although respondents felt strongly that the relocation process is more difficult for blacks, I attempted to discover whether or not there might be some factors that would ease the difficulties associated with relocation. Inherent in my line of reasoning was the assumption that there exists a black middle-class "community," not in a geographic sense but as a community of collective consciousness and responsibilities, small but active, that black corporate managers are part of. My hypothesis, that in some ways relocation is easier for blacks because they are part of a "closed community" or black middle-class network, although not entirely born out, enabled me to identify those factors that are helpful in making the adjustment to relocation occur more smoothly. Although subjective, appraisals of whether relocation is easier for blacks were mostly negative, subjects' responses to a variety of other questions suggested that there were resources in the black community that blacks could turn to for assistance or support.[1]

The focus for assessing and measuring adjustment to relocation for managers and their families was the identification of factors aiding in establishing new friendships and a new social network on relocation. Three such factors were identified and used as the basis for assessment. They are (a) the existence of factors such as "informal networking" as operationalized by referral from friends; (b) subjects' membership and participation in civic, social, and fraternal organizations; and (c) participation in organized religion and church activities.

Respondents cited informal networking as the most frequent way of making social contacts in the new location. It is reasonable to conclude that the small size of the black professional population in our society facilitates this, particularly on relocation to major cities (including the surrounding suburbs), which are where most blacks reside. The colloquial humorism, that all blacks with college degrees know each other, is not far from the truth. In addition, the realization that the professional black community is so small, and the difficulties in establishing relationships with other blacks in that social strata inherent in this fact, create a willingness within this small group to foster social relations among others via introducing newcomers to their social network. Often these networks are quite extensive in numbers and cut across geographic areas in scope. There exist elements of *gemeinschaft* resembling Tönnies's (1957) original description of the concept of the cooperative and interdependent nature of social relations within the black middle-class community.

This is an interesting finding. Its importance lies in its uniqueness to the black experience. In a small white sample collected in tandem with this study ($N = 19$), respondents identified work as the primary source of new friendships on relocation to a new city or town. This was not found to be the case among the black respondents. The large majority of blacks ranked work third in order of importance when asked to give the three most important sources of new friendships, which is consistent with the findings of Fernandez (1981). Work does not appear to function for blacks in the establishment of social relationships to the same extent or with the same strength that it does for whites. It is not as important among blacks in providing relationships of a more personal, intimate nature as is typically associated with friendship. This is in part due to the social isolation of blacks in the corporate workplace, and most indicated that those work associates with whom they socialized away from the office, apart from work-related functions, or both were most often black. Finally, to some extent, there is a desire to separate work from leisure, and the view that work and leisure are separate spheres.[2]

Another important resource for blacks relocating is black civic, social, and fraternal organizations. Most respondents in the sample claimed membership in one or more of these national organizations. About a quarter of respondents were members of black sororities or fraternities. Those few respondents who were not members of any black civic, social, or fraternal organizations said that they participated in the activities of these organizations. Thus, all respondents had some level of involvement with these organizations. All respondents stated that these organizations were helpful in their making new acquaintances, finding sources of entertainment and leisure activities, building new informal support systems, and becoming engaged in the new community.

A sizable number of respondents (162, $N = 191$) indicated that they are regular churchgoers. Regular church attendance was defined on the basis of attending a church service at least once per month, although many in the sample attended weekly. In addition to attending Sunday service, a smaller number mentioned being active in the men's or women's group of their church, being deacons in the church, serving as members of the church council, or participants in church social functions. Church membership and participating in various church activities serve not only as an important source of spiritual support, but also as a social outlet and an avenue to involvement in community life.

Regular church attendance by such a large number of the managers and their wives interviewed may seem surprising. We could have reasonably speculated, as others have done, that with the rise of middle- and upper-middle-class status the rate of regular church attendance would diminish and be lower than for working-class or lower-middle-class groups. Church attendance decreases as socioeconomic status (SES) increases—an artifact of higher levels of educational attainment within high-SES groups. Although this study does not allow for comparisons across class lines, it can be concluded on the basis of these findings that there is a high rate of regular church attendance among middle-class black managers and their families. Furthermore, for most respondents who rated the importance of church in their lives and the lives of their families, the responses ranged from *important* to *very important*.

In summary, we can say then that black managerial families "on the move" have some supports to help them to develop a sense of social connectedness in the communities to which they relocate. The majority of respondents in the sample use one or all of these supports when they relocate. This does not imply that the relocation experience is not difficult for blacks, or that the experience is easier for blacks than for whites, for this is not the case. There are, however, some factors within the black community that might be considered "helps" that mitigate the stresses of relocation.

THE PROBLEMS ENCOUNTERED: THE DETAILS
MAY DIFFER BUT MOST TELL A SIMILAR TALE

In a study by Margolis (1979) of white corporate families, homogeneity among its residents was found to be an important factor in the selection of the community in which the family would reside on relocation to a new region. Although all families, black and white, have a concern for reestablishing roots in the new community, the specific criteria used in choosing a new community are somewhat different.

Margolis (1979) found that her subjects sought homogeneous communities to minimize the social distance between their family and their neighbors. The underlying thinking was that by moving into a neighborhood in which all of the people were very much the same, the transition to the new neighborhood would be easier, and they could more quickly and easily become entrenched in the new community. The desire for homogeneity was carried out to the point of matching themselves with the other residents by race, age, ages of the children, type of cars driven, type of occupation, and even the company or companies the neighbors worked for.

This is not the case with blacks. Among the black corporate families in this sample, homogeneity of the neighborhood was not a criterion for selection in any respect. Although blacks were often attracted to those geographic areas that had at least some black residents, in the specific neighborhood they chose race really did not factor into the decision. They were concerned about the neighborhoods they selected less because of the people who lived in them and more for what the neighborhood and community had to offer. The criteria for selection of a neighborhood included such things as the quality of the schools, available services, home resale values, with emphasis placed on the individual house itself. Managers and their spouses took it as a given that they would simply commute to visit friends and transport their children to do the same. The possibilities for the development of social relationships on any level within the neighborhood were not important.

They did, however, hope that their experiences with racism in the new community, including overt prejudice, stereotyping, differential treatment, and harassment, would be few or nonexistent. Unfortunately, for most this was not the case. A few managers and their family members experienced incidents of extreme racism. Others experienced less extreme encounters. All had a story to tell.

At a 2-day conference sponsored by the black employees' caucus of one of the corporations represented in the study, in between workshops I spoke informally with a small group of managers' wives. I casually asked the question "Have any of you had experiences with racism in any of the communities to which you've relocated?" Among the responses, one right after another, were "Of course." "Certainly." "How long do we have before we have to get back?" (to the workshop). One woman simply looked at me as if to say, "How incredibly naive you are to even have to ask such a question!" Then they proceeded to tell of their experiences.

A brown-complected, middle-aged woman said, "I am so tired of people ringing my doorbell and asking me if the lady of the house is in." (They presume that she is the maid!)

Another woman told of her next-door neighbor's comments about her and her husband being so industrious based on the neighbor's observations of them cutting the lawn and taking in the trash cans after trash collection. These routines, considered usual for any middle-class homeowner, were viewed as remarkable, for some reason, for blacks.

One woman, ordering meats from the local butcher shop, reading off from the grocery list in her hand, asked for a crown rib roast. When the butcher said that they had none, she replied that she would take a sirloin roast instead. The butcher told her that she had better check on that first because the two were very different. She asked him, "Check with whom!?" He replied, "The lady that you're shopping for." She was outraged because she was shopping with her own list for meats for her own family.

Had there not been a full agenda of conference activities planned for that afternoon, I suspect that these discussions would have continued for several hours.

In the context of the interviews with my sample of corporate spouses, this same line of inquiry was pursued. Many of the respondents had interesting, although amazing and disheartening stories to tell. Some of them follow.

Carmelle Clark

Married for 13 years to manager Melvin Clark, Carmelle is a part-time special education teacher and mother of three children. The Clarks relocated shortly after the birth of their third child. The incident that she relates occurred only a couple of weeks after moving into their new home.

One morning, while Mrs. Clark was having breakfast with her two older children and feeding her infant, the housekeeper whom they had recently hired informed her that several minutes ago she may have set off the silent alarm system by opening a back door before checking to see if the system was disarmed. Mrs. Clark telephoned the police but was too late to head off the squad car responding to the alarm. When the police arrived, the housekeeper let them in and led them into the kitchen, where they found Mrs. Clark and her children seated at the breakfast table still in their pajamas and bathrobes. Mrs. Clark apologized for the false alarm and attempted to explain that they were all new to the house and unaccustomed to the system, but was cut off and was ordered to provide some evidence of proof of residence. She was able to quickly produce a copy of the mortgage contract because she had just received it from her attorney. This was not sufficient. The police officers wanted to see photo identification! She produced her driver's license with her picture on it. Mrs. Clark recalls standing mortified in her night-clothes, having to justify her existence to the two white officers. She then had to discuss the incident with her children, who were upset and confused by the presence of police in their house, confronting their mother in their sharp tones of voice.

Although one can appreciate the precautions taken by the police to protect a home from being robbed, it also seems apparent that a robbery was not taking place in this instance. Two women and three small children wearing pajamas and eating breakfast is not the usual modus operandi for burglars. One can only assume that the two police officers, because of their adherence to stereotypes about blacks—that they are all poor, or criminals—found it incredible that a black family would be living in a nice home in an upper-middle-class community, engaging in normal family behaviors. Although comforted by the quick response to the triggered alarm, Mrs. Clark was also disheartened and disappointed by this "welcome" to her new neighborhood.

Senita and Stanley Jordan

This successful young black manager and his wife moved to an upper-middle-class community in Fairfield County, Connecticut. Realizing their long-time dream, they purchased their first home, a condominium presently valued at about $200,000. After 12 years with his company, Jordan drives a medium-priced but new automobile and is notably well dressed.

After living in their condo for about a year, they were burglarized while both were out of town on business trips. On their return, their next-door neighbors (white) informed the couple that they had seen two shady-looking characters, white males dressed in shabby clothing and unkempt in appearance (very unlike the usual visitors that the Jordans receive), driving a truck, loitering outside of the Jordans' home as they (the neighbors) were leaving for an afternoon walk. They also observed that the door to the couple's home was open. The neighbors were aware that the Jordans were out of town and told the two men that the Jordans would return after a certain hour that afternoon. When the neighbors returned from their walk they once again found the door to the Jordans' home open and the house burglarized. Jordan and his wife, who suffered losses of approximately $14,000 in theft, were quite upset by their loss and the invasion of their privacy. Although they did not voice their feelings, they could not understand why their neighbors had not called the police immediately when they observed what they described in their own words as "suspicious" circumstances.

Some months later, one of these neighbors rang their doorbell, saying that she needed to clear her conscience of something that was troubling her. She had just come from a "meditation-sharing" session with some other neighbors in which she talked about the incident of the Jordan burglary. They urged her to share her feelings with the Jordans. She explained to the couple that she saw them as young (the implication being "too" young, although both are in their 30s) and very "successful," and because of Stanley Jordan's frequent travel and sometimes late work hours she assumed, despite the fact that he had told them that he was a manager with a major corporation, that he was a drug dealer. She therefore did not want to call the police, although she suspected that a burglary was taking place, because she thought that drugs might be discovered in the house and she did not want to be the cause of the couple being arrested! She was certain that the Jordans thought that she was stupid for not realizing that the two suspicious characters who robbed the place were up to no good. She was relieved to get this off of her chest.

The Jordans, who thought of the neighbors as friends, were reminded that racism is "alive and well" in the United States, and were both saddened and angered by the fact that their loss and the trauma associated with the incident could have been prevented. It seems obvious that if an identical couple, with all of the same behaviors and attributes except race, were in this scenario, the neighbors would not have assumed the worst—that the Jordans were of illicit means and reaped their livelihood through criminal activity. I am certain that the average upwardly mobile young middle-class couple who buys a condominium in the suburbs, owns a Japanese import car, and wears well-tailored business suits is not assumed by their neighbors to be drug dealers. (Rather, I believe they are called "yuppies.") It seems clear that this was a racist incident, which would not have occurred had the couple been white.

Conclusion

Relocation is a stressful experience for all families; however, it poses special problems for black families. Specifically, two problem areas or sources of stress identified for black corporate managerial families, the subjects of this research, were social isolation and physical distancing from kin support networks. The geographic mobility that can be assumed with upward mobility in corporate employment pulls blacks to areas where often there are few other blacks and few black cultural supports, and makes it difficult to maintain family ties that have been historically seen as a source of support crucial to the very survival of African Americans.

The respondents felt that although relocation was much more difficult for black versus white families, resources within the black community function to ease the experience. Three support factors were identified. Informal networking via referrals from friends, membership and/or participation in the activities of black civic, social, and fraternal organizations, and participation in church activities all served as potential sources for new friendships and social relations. Most individuals and families use these resources on relocating. In an overriding sense, we can conclude that racism is a major factor affecting black families on the move, whether that move takes them across the country or merely to a more affluent neighborhood in the same community. Racism was identified as a significant concern among the managers and their spouses. Their hope was that experiences with racism in their new communities would be limited because many had disheartening stories to share of previous personal experiences with racism.

The next chapter focuses on the other women in this study: the wives of black corporate managers.

Notes

1. Testing of the hypothesis would provide credence for the validity of the assumption that there exists a black middle-class "community."

2. This perspective holds implications for the viewing of work and family life as separate entities. Although this is in contradiction to the traditional notion of the "corporate family," we have seen an increasing tendency toward a shift in thinking in this direction, especially among new corporate workers.

7

The Incorporation of Wives
in Husbands' Work

If I were single, I would not have moved as often and would
be further along in my career. My career has suffered greatly.
—Cynthia Daniels, middle-aged corporate wife of 25 years

It has been asserted that with their married male managers, the corporation gets two workers for the price of one. That is, wives of corporate managers support their husbands' careers in a variety of subtle as well as overt ways. We also must observe that the nature of this support is both direct as well as indirect. Although it has been said that the traditional notion of the corporate wife is changing (Fernandez, 1981), this investigation concludes that wives' incorporation still persists among corporate wives—including black corporate wives. In the next several pages I will focus briefly on

- the concept of wives' incorporation;
- the changing nature of incorporation; and
- special issues of incorporation as related to black wives.

The ultimate analysis of the concept in this chapter will occur in the context of this final point in reference to incorporation.

The Meaning of Wives' Incorporation

The concept of wives' incorporation in men's work had its origins in the work of Papanek (1973). In her article, she begins the professional discussion of the two-person career by asserting that the traditional stereotype of the wifely role is extended to further complement the work roles of men. This takes place in the form of adding to the volume of her duties as wife as supporter, home manager, chief child-rearer, and entertainer (e.g., through entertaining work associates). Papanek also asserts that the involvement of women in the two-person career also functions as a social control mechanism that averts the career aspirations of women by involving them informally in their husbands' jobs. She delimits wives' incorporation as a particularly middle-class phenomenon and thus one that has more relevance in the lives of educated married women. Wives are pulled into participating in the two-person career through their economic, emotional, and sexual ties to their husbands. They are rewarded for their efforts via vicarious achievement through the husband's success (or suffer achievement deprivation if he is not successful) and are paid for their work vicariously through their husband's paycheck. In some cases, such vicarious achievement is built into the structure of the middle-class wife's role rather than being something that occurs by chance. As Papanek states, wives are "gainfully unemployed" and "gainfully" occupied.

The concept of incorporation seems particularly lendable to corporate families. Although professional writings have seldom pinned a name to the phenomenon, it has been described in numerous works focusing on corporate managers and their wives (see Kanter, 1977; Seidenberg, 1973; Vandervelde, 1979; Whyte, 1951a, 1951b). In fact, Papanek (1973) tells us, "The best-known two-person career pattern is that of the corporate executive's wife" (p. 858).

WHAT IS A "CORPORATE WIFE"?

The "corporate wife" as a social role was first looked at in the early 1950s by William H. Whyte, who published a series of articles in *Fortune* magazine, as well as other writings. Whyte and others of the time portrayed these wives as helpless victims confined to household chores and lacking their husbands' opportunities for learning and achievement. The role was characterized by a lack of autonomy. Although there were benefits associated with the role, according to Kanter (1977), "Marriage to successful men was constraining, shaped role demand for wives, and often put the family last in men's priorities" (p. 110).

There are many ways in which the manager's wife participates as an unofficial (and even sometimes official) part of the corporation. Of course, there is variation in the extent to which individual wives view the corporation as part of their lives, but there are numerous variables that tie most wives into corporate participation on some level. Among these variables are the following: the expectation on the part of the corporation that the manager's wife participate socially in corporate-related functions; the corporate expectations that the husband be on 24-hour call to allow for out-of-town travel and late work hours (the wife must pick up the slack by assuming his household and familial responsibilities); mainstream U.S. gender roles, which prescribe a supportive and subordinate role to that of the husband and his career, and delegate primary responsibility for the domestic sphere to the wife; and the limited avenues for women's achievement with respect to self-esteem, job status, and income in contemporary society.

Today, it is still especially difficult to categorize exactly where wives fit into the corporation or how to characterize them as both insiders and outsiders as the role of the corporate wife diminishes. There is no uniformity in their participation. For some, they are involved directly and/or indirectly through their husbands, and for others, almost not at all. The latter holds true for many of the younger corporate wives (those under 30) who because of their own career demands are less likely, less able, and less interested in having high involvement in their husbands' corporate activities. Also, corporations vary in their expectations of wives—ranging from high expectations to virtually none at all. Thus, the problem of defining the situation of the corporate wife becomes even more difficult.

Wives' sentiments vary with respect to how they feel about the presence of the corporation in their lives and that of their family, and, in turn, how much they accepted or resisted the corporation's influence. Some wives are accepting of corporate demands and view corporate presence as a powerful factor in shaping their lives. Kanter (1977) writes, "From the wives' perspective, the company was a critical part of their lives, defining how they spent their time and influencing what was possible in their relationships with their husbands" (p. 105).

Other wives identify their involvement with the corporation as opportunities lost to them because of their involvement and their direct services to the corporation. Of these, some resented the loss of personal opportunities, and see themselves as unpaid workers for the corporation. Their sentiments reinforce Finch's (1983) conceptualization of the impact of husbands' work on the lives of their wives—"a man's work imposes a set of structures *upon* his wife's life consequently, constrains her choices about the living of her own life, and sets limits upon what is possible for her" (p. 2, emphasis in the original). Incorporation then, must be viewed both as women's contributions to their husbands' work as well as the external constraints imposed on women through the ways in which husbands' work structures women's lives. Finch calls this a "two-way relationship." Others were willing to make the sacrifice, in part because of the ultimate rewards they received via their husbands' employment in the corporation. Finally, some wives are most resentful of what they perceived to be the intrusion of the corporation in their personal lives. They resist the notion of the corporation getting more and more involved in their workers' private lives.

My research findings show that these wives tend to be women with their own careers and therefore do not have the need for a closed corporate social community or the tangible by-products of corporate paternalism. To the extent that wives' participation in the corporation is voluntary, varying wifely sentiment affects the degree and quality of wives' participation, for example, those who are most resentful tend to participate less in supporting their husbands' work role, especially in those ways that are not mandatory or absolutely expected.

There are other problems that ensue for women from the notion that men bring two workers to the job. (Women bring one, or even less). Among them is the fact that the corporate relationship is one-sided. There has been a double standard of participation. The corporation dictates that wives be included in the corporation in some ways, but left out in other respects. Wives don't have a voice, but are sometimes called on to serve. Thus, there is a lack of reciprocity of power and reward for women in their relation to their husbands' corporation. The traditional corporate wife, in a sense, is a voiceless victim without recourse and lacking power.

How specifically do wives participate in their husbands' work lives? Kanter (1977, p. 110) has classified four primary ways in which wives contribute to husbands and their work:

1. "Direct substitution" (for his secretary—typing, answering the telephone, helping to make contacts);

2. "indirect support" (hostessing, which is part of the content of the "wifely" social role, but for business-related purposes);
3. "consulting" (gives business advice, serves as listener); and
4. "emotional aid" (again, part of the "wifely" role, keeping the husband in good spirits, being available to him as a sounding board.

In addition to these four areas in which the corporate wife may serve as a helpmate, we must recognize the ways in which she assists him with his domestic or familial responsibilities, which he, on a frequent or infrequent basis, is unable to fulfill because of the demands of the job. Specifically, the wife may serve as surrogate father in times of his absence, taking children to lessons or club meetings, or with other functions that the family has identified as his responsibility; assume full-time rather than shared parenting[1] responsibility; and assume his household chores such as yard work, a responsibility that corporate managers and their wives typically identified as being the husband's. This category of help would appear to be at least as important as those identified previously because it is the very thing that allows the husband the independence to pursue a career, and to enjoy all of the positive benefits associated with it, and at the same time enjoy the comforts, pleasures, and stability of family life. Wives contribute to men's work through various types of support, both related to the job and in the domestic affectional sphere. Thus, wives' incorporation in men's work not only assists men in maintaining and enhancing their occupational role, but also in maintaining their family role. By wives supporting men in their roles, men are bolstered and better perform in their various roles. Wives enable men to "have their cake and eat it, too." This very important aspect of incorporation may be less apparent due to traditional sex role biases and the false assertion that home and work are separate spheres.

THE DIMINISHING ROLE OF THE CORPORATE SPOUSE

Social changes of recent years have caused the role of the corporate wife to diminish in reference to her level of participation in her husband's career. Both the contemporary women's movement and the sexual revolution have encouraged women to pursue social roles apart from the dominant sphere, and have eaten away at the notion that the role of women in the family is subservient to the role of men. These changes have culminated in women pursuing educational opportunities and careers such that today the majority of U.S. women, regardless of marital status, work outside of the home, and in sex roles becoming more egalitarian and flexible so that household responsibilities are shared.

In the wake of these changes, the traditional corporate spouse role has changed. Some, in fact, have asserted that the role of the corporate spouse is vanishing (Dransfield, 1984). We can indeed say that the "new" corporate spouse is younger and has been socialized in the "liberated woman" era, is more likely to have a career, and is not likely in every case to be female with the rise in female corporate managers. All of these changes in the corporate spouse profile have had an impact on the corporate spouse role.

Corporations are unsure of how much they can expect of the spouse today. Changes in the family including new patterns of marriage (marrying later than we did in recent past years, and the high divorce and remarriage rates), courtship, living arrangements, and dual careerism contribute to the corporation's lessening demand for spouse participation. From this angle, one might perceive that there is less of a need for the traditional corporate spouse, and that wives' incorporation is all but a thing of the past.

Let's return to our focus on wives' incorporation. I would like to assert that the phenomenon of wives' incorporation can be defined as occurring on four levels:

1. Direct participation in husband's career (secretarial assistance, hostessing, and social partner);
2. emotional support;
3. freeing the husband of domestic responsibilities and family duties; and
4. the loss of opportunity to the wife.

This list differs from Kanter's (1977) in that her first two ways of support ("direct substitution" and "indirect support") are collapsed into one category and are perceived of as essentially similar types of support, as is also the case with Kanter's third and fourth ways ("consulting" and "emotional aid"). The distinctions within these pairs are less significant than are their similarities. But, more important, this newly devised list includes support on two levels not included on Kanter's list—relating to domestic responsibilities and wife's opportunities lost.

If we accept a multileveled definition of the phenomenon, it is apparent that the most easy to observe aspects of the phenomenon involve only the first level of incorporation, the more social or public level. It would take closer scrutiny, a look at the private domain, to discern whether wives were involved on other levels. Although incorporation on the first level is discernible by the casual observer, a closer look at corporate families and the intimacies of their interactions is necessary if we are to get the full flavor of how wives are involved.

The assessment that the role of the corporate wife is vanishing, and that the phenomenon of incorporation is one that will fade away with the older generation of corporate spouses, appears to be based on the decrease in wives' participation in the husband's work on the first more social level. Indeed, corporate wives report that they entertain their husbands' business associates less frequently than did corporate spouses in decades past. The number of company-sponsored functions to which wives are invited is also decreasing. Only a very rare few reported having any involvement in secretarial-type activities.[2] But this type of involvement pertains to only one level of incorporation. A more intimate look at the private lives of male corporate manager and their wives tells a different story. The findings of this study support the fact that wives' incorporation in their husbands' work is alive and well in corporate America—especially on the less social, more private levels.

The Context of Incorporation for Black Wives

My interviews yielded some interesting black wifely perspectives on the phenomenon of wives' incorporation. But before going further, I must comment that the phenomenon of wives' incorporation is one to which these wives for the most part would not relate. Younger women see themselves as independent, and free from the sex role restrictions that previous generations of women in our society were subject to. For older women, a generational factor is operative. That is, the behaviors of wives' incorporation are merely a part of the content of the roles associated with the status of wife.

The negative connotations of wives' incorporation are not always perceptible to U.S. women regardless of race because the content of the phenomenon is consistent with traditional sex role prescriptions for women in our society. And although black women function with their own subcultural sex role prescriptions, they are also subject to mainstream sex role norms, so that both groups of women, black and white, see it as their role to exhibit the behaviors that are the content of wives' incorporation. Although I would hypothesize that the concept is one that would not be claimed by white corporate wives either, there are some differences between the two groups of women as to why they may not readily identify with the notion of wives' incorporation. Let us explore some of these.

There are several factors that are part of the content of black U.S. culture that are relevant to black wifely views of how they should function in the family context. Black women's perspectives on incorporation must be viewed in light of the following factors:

— traditional values on childbearing and the prevailing cultural idea of a woman's place in the family context (when financially feasible)
— group versus individual orientation
— role flexibility may equal or equate with the wife taking over husband's responsibilities

Traditional values on childbearing and homemaking have always seen women as the ones in charge of these spheres. Despite the fact that economic conditions within the black family often make it appear otherwise, black women's primary role is that of caretaker of the domestic sphere. When economic conditions permit, when it can be afforded (e.g., when families have reached solid middle-class status) this is the cultural value that is upheld.

Another factor is the group versus individual orientation pervasive in the black community. Although white wives have complained about a lack of their own fulfillment because of sacrifices they had to make because of their husbands' careers (see Seidenberg, 1973), black women did not complain about what they had to give up personally but felt comfortable with their decisions to defer to their husbands' careers, and felt that their decisions and personal sacrifices were in the best interest of the family. This was especially true of the younger wives that I interviewed. Two things are important here: These women felt that they had some control, that they had a choice to make, even to the extent that they chose to accept the sex role prescription for women to support their husbands, and that the good of the whole is what was most important. The black wife positively perceived her role as a responsible, independent, strong woman, as shaping her own behaviors and making decisions for herself that are in the family's best interest. Her perception of her own success thus is intimately tied to the success of her family.[3]

Finally, if we refer back to the black family strength of role flexibility within the family that was discussed in Chapter 2, we find another hint as to how black women view the elements of incorporation in their lives. In the same way that we have said that the valued role of women in the black family is that of caretaker in the domestic role despite the fact that economic situations fostered by racism and discrimination dictated that she at times serve as the primary or a primary breadwinner, so too must she flex to assume some of her husband's other functions or responsibilities in response to his work demands. Again, whatever is in the best interest of the family, whatever is necessary for survival is what must occur. The corporate wife's attitude toward her role of wife and mother, in a very real sense, appears to be a feminist one in its degree of perceived self-determination. This was especially true among the younger, under age 40 corporate wives.

At the same time, we cannot ignore a small degree of being unfulfilled among some older black corporate wives who because of their sex, in their earlier developmental years, had fewer options for fulfillment apart from their family roles. Although they do not exhibit anywhere near the same degree of resentment as can be found in earlier studies of white corporate wives of their generation or age cohort (see Archer, 1969; Kanter, 1977; Seidenberg, 1973), they are aware that their own personal growth was stunted compared with their husbands'—which flourished.

Findings

All wives indicated having some level of (direct) participation in their husbands' business-related social activities. The participation rates for entertaining husband's business associates ranged from 1 to 12 times yearly, the modal average being 2 to 4. The rate of attending company-sponsored functions ranged from 2 to 24 or more times per year, the average being 4 to 6 times per year. All wives indicated that they attended these functions whenever possible, and for most this equals 100% participation in those functions to which they were invited. It is interesting to note that the decrease in wives' participation is directly related to the decrease in company demand. As corporations extend fewer invitations to wives, wives have fewer to accept.

On the level of emotional support, most wives supported their husbands on all measures in this category. The wives said they often verbally express their pride in their husbands (68%); they frequently act as sounding boards for their husbands (72%); 86% said that they generally understand the frustrations of their husbands' work; and a full 100% said that they feel they are supportive of husband and his work.

We see that the data informs us that wives are still very much incorporated in their husbands' work lives, although this is less apparent due to the decrease in public forms of incorporation behaviors. (Although a few wives indicated that they have directly supported their husbands' work, for example, doing typing for them on an occasional basis, the extent of this behavior was not sufficient enough to warrant mention.)

Wives indicated a high level of incorporation in freeing husbands from responsibility for domestic and family duties, which they were sometimes unable to perform because of time spent on the job. Of all the wives, 97% admitted to engaging in at least one form of this behavior, including assuming ultimate responsibility for child care if both must work late (48%) or travel out of town (92%), and having the bulk of responsibility for family and domestic functions on a regular basis (72%). Although most indicated that their husbands did share in the household chores (91%) and performed some family and domestic chores on a regular basis, they also said that they sometimes had to assume the husband's duties if work responsibilities prevented him from performing them (52%). It is interesting to note that husbands tended to have a greater perception of the amount of responsibility they assume in the household than the perception of husband's responsibility held by the wife. Thus, we have a discrepancy in wife's versus husband's views of their assessment of the extent of husband's participation in domestic chores.

Wives tend to be less aware of incorporation on this level, perhaps because we are dealing with deeply embedded traditional role responsibilities. Although one might say that consciousness has not been raised to this level of awareness in reference to incorporation, we must also recognize a willingness on the part of these wives to do what is in the best interest of the family.

Nearly all wives admitted that they had experienced a loss of personal career opportunity because they have supported their husbands' careers. Of the wives, 94% indicated that they would be further along in their career if they were single. Several mentioned changing to, or choosing, a career that was family compatible. Barbara Brown, Hilda Roland, and

Cynthia Daniels are three such women. Their stories illustrate the range of sentiment among black corporate wives on this issue.

Barbara Brown is 36 years old, has been married for 12 years, and is the mother of two small children. She has been with her husband since the beginning of his career and they have had to relocate about once every 2 years, although they have been in their present location nearly 4 years. Having earned a master's degree, Barbara has bounced back and forth between the job fields of education and personnel, working for 8 years in education and 6 years in personnel because of her husband's job relocations. She has been in her present job for approximately one year but it took nearly 3 years for her to land a job in what can be considered close to her field. For Barbara, family comes first. She has modified her career field from corporate personnel to personnel in education because it gives her more regular hours and allows her more time to care for family. She says that this was a hard decision to make, but it is best while the children are young. She appears to be happy and says that she is enjoying her life. According to Barbara, "It's really not much of a sacrifice when I consider the benefits for my family."

Hilda Roland, married to Charles Roland for 8 years, is 30 years old. The couple met in college and married after Hilda's graduation (Charles was a few years ahead of Hilda in school). She is from a strong family background, and because of her father being a noted educator, Hilda received a lot of support and encouragement in her studies from childhood. She is active in sports as is her husband and has many hobbies.

Hilda studied communications in college and found the field to be very interesting. She decided that she wanted a career in television production. While in college she interned at a local television station and found the experience to be more than rewarding.

After graduation, she moved to another city to join Charles. With no job leads in the new city, Hilda spent nearly 4 months finding a job in her field. A new television station was opening and hired her as a production assistant. Within a year, Hilda was given a raise and was promised the next assistant producer position that came available at the station.

In the meantime, Charles was moving up his career ladder. He received a promotion and was temporarily relocated for a period of about 2 years in the new assignment. Hilda took a job in a children's media center. When Charles was transferred back to their previous location, she was rehired by the television station, but in community affairs rather than in production; and, at first, she was allowed to work only part-time. Approximately 3 years later, Charles was once again promoted and re-assigned. Hilda had difficulty finding her job with her present company. She is working at a small cable network and has once again had to change departments. She says that there is not much room for growth in the company and that she does not have much in common with the people she works with. Hilda says, "I'm in the position where I don't exactly look forward to going into work each day. I've been job-hunting recently but have not had much luck and I'm now considering [starting] some kind of business." She goes on to say that she considers herself to be successful but not as successful as she knows she can be.

I must preface the next wife's story by saying that she is more resentful of opportunities lost to her because of husband's career and more angry than most in the older wives cohort. Only one other wife said that she was somewhat resentful of opportunities lost, although a few said that careerwise they were doing not quite as well as they expected.

Cynthia Daniels is 49 years old and has been a corporate wife for 25 years. She has a master's degree in library science and has worked part-time for the past several years after the children were both in high school and now college.

In her estimation, she is not doing as well as she expected careerwise. Cynthia feels that her husband's career prevented her from achieving her career aspirations. She does not consider herself to be successful because she has not met her career goals. But she does not see herself as different from her peers, siblings, or those with whom she grew up in this regard. Cynthia says, "If I were single, I would not have moved as often and would be further along in my career. My career has suffered greatly." In recollecting the early years of her marriage, she says that there were times when she was not always happy, and was sometimes lonely.

PROFILE OF THE YOUNGER COHORT OF WIVES

The younger age cohort of wives in the sample (women in their mid- to late 30s or younger) are very similar to Barbara Brown. They are college graduates, and some have graduate degrees. All are employed in what can be called professional, managerial, or administrative jobs. They have put their family responsibilities first, although they take their careers very seriously, and career is often a close competitor with family for their time and energies. They often switched to jobs or chose career spheres such as teaching, which were compatible with caring for a family, although a few, like their husbands, are also corporate managers. Nearly all have children, or plan to.

They share in the ups and downs of their husbands' work, and try to be involved and supportive. Although these wives occasionally complain about the long work hours that their husbands put in, taking away time that the family could spend together, they are generally accepting and understanding. One could say that their approach to husband's work is, "We're in this together." They are good team players.

In their view, the corporation definitely still has expectations of them as wives. Many feel that the corporation is 20 years behind the times in this regard. Although they are not enamored with having to attend their husbands' company social functions, neither are they resentful. They are willing to participate to support their husbands and do so whenever asked.

I would describe them as a group as happy, self-assured, and proactive in playing a role in shaping the forces that affect their lives.

ASSESSMENT OF THE POST-40 WIVES COHORT

The post-40 age cohort of wives had many similarities with the younger cohort of wives, but at the same time, they were distinctive in some ways. They were similar with respect to being highly educated, being supportive of husband and his career, and in placing a strong importance on family. They differed in that they felt they had made more personal sacrifices because of husband's career.

Few of these women were longtime career women. Many did not work or only worked part-time until their children were grown. They felt that they had given up more in their careers than did the younger cohort. When asked if they thought they were unusual compared with other black corporate wives of their generation, they said they were not.

Among these longtime veteran wives, although with not quite the same air of independence or sense that their lives were ones of choice as found in the younger cohort, these women felt that the sacrifices they had made were in the interest of husband and family and therefore had been worth it. They assessed their personal success by their family success. They are unlike their white age cohort of corporate wives in that they are more accepting of what they had to give up because of husband's career and seemed to evaluate their degree of personal success more positively, and more by family success (see Kanter, 1977; Seidenberg, 1973; Vandervelde, 1979).

THE BLACK CORPORATE WIFE OF THE '90S AND BEYOND

Patricia Bellwood, one among the cohort of younger wives, is both typical of this group and at the same time a superstar among them. In addition to being a corporate wife, she is a successful corporate manager. But, like many wives in the sample, her career plans were altered in deference to her husband's career. For Bellwood, family comes first. Her overall personal success is measured largely by family success and she feels that the sacrifices she has made have been her choice, and well worth it in the best interest of her family. She adheres to fairly traditional gender role norms regarding her family roles of wife and mother. With respect to the concept of wives' incorporation, she supports her husband in both his work and family roles. Her family of origin was important in contributing to her success. Although she sometimes feels the pressure of juggling work and family roles, she seems to manage well and is generally happy.

Profile: Patricia Bellwood

I found Patricia to be an especially impressive young woman, as were many in the sample. The mother of two children, Bellwood, age 35, has been married for 5 ½ years. Both she and her husband are employed in corporate managerial jobs. She has been a corporate employee for 12 years and is a college graduate. Bellwood earns in excess of $60,000 per year. We should note that Bellwood did not marry until age 29, which gave her several years to invest all of her energies in her work, moving full steam ahead in her career. She married Charles Bellwood at a point when she was very well established in her particular area of management.

Bellwood does differ from other women in the sample in that her father was a corporate person. When asked how she chose corporate life rather than some other career path, she admitted that because of her father's involvement in corporate employ, this was a familiar one to her. Although she had prepared to be a teacher and did spend her earlier career years employed as a teacher, low pay and being assigned to unsafe neighborhood schools caused her to seek another line of work. Her father's experience in corporate America made this an easy choice for her. It also suggests that in marrying her husband she had a role model in her mother to exemplify what the role of a corporate wife entails.

As a student, Patricia excelled. She expressed that her family was very important in her educational development and that both parents supported and encouraged her in her studies. She spends her leisure time playing tennis, skiing, and reading. Her extra money is spent on decorating her home, recreation, clothing, and eating out.

Part of what I found to be impressive about this young woman was her striking physical appearance—that she is extremely well groomed, extremely well composed, and very personable. But what was most striking about Bellwood was her assertiveness, her positive sense of self-esteem, and most important, her sense of independence. I would describe Patricia Bellwood as a superwoman—one who tries to excel in career, as a wife, as a homemaker, and as a mother. Although she has had to make some sacrifices, she takes responsibility for the choices that she has made in her life, and she did choose after pursuing a career as a single woman to take on the responsibility of a husband and a family. Her career is extremely important to her; however, she makes her role as wife and mother a priority. But she feels self-assuredly that this was her choice to make. In a sense, Patricia Bellwood might see herself as somewhat of a feminist, or a "liberated woman," from the standpoint that her life is of her own making. She has come a long way from prior generations of black women. It was her decision to take on her heavyweight work and family roles. At the same time, if an outsider were to dig a little bit deeper into Bellwood's life, they would see indicators that her career has been stymied as a result of what she considers to have been her conscious choices to care for family.

Patricia is extremely child oriented even though neither of the children is her biological offspring. Patricia works late on the average of three evenings per week, but also indicated that she tries to be home before her husband, and this is almost always the case. She has approximately 10 out-of-town business trips per year. Her mother takes care of the children when she has to work especially late or when she travels out of town. It is interesting to note that it is Patricia's mother who cares for the children in light of the fact that these are not Patricia's biological offspring but her husband's. This would seem to be in keeping with the involvement of blacks in surrogate parenting networks and roles in Patricia's viewing these children as her own, and in Patricia's mother also taking on a surrogate grandparenting role. It may also be indicative of the adherence to traditional sex role norms for women in the black community and mainstream U.S. culture. Patricia said that when both she and Charles have to travel out of town overnight, she will first try to reschedule her travel and if she is unsuccessful, again, her mother will care for the children. Although Charles is very involved with and caring of his children, Patricia perceives that the day-to-day responsibility for them rests on her.

Patricia has said that she aspires to upward mobility in her company, but if she were offered a promotion in another city, she would definitely have to defer to Charles and to Charles's job situation. It would also have to be not just a lateral move for Charles but a promotion for Charles as well. This family has relocated during the 5 ½ tenure of their marriage on the basis of Charles having received a promotion. She has generally been accepting of this and rationalized to me very matter-of-factly that because Charles is the major breadwinner in the family and his company takes care of their moving needs (expenses, packing, and so on), she has been relatively accepting of the relocation opportunities. Patricia was reluctant to admit that she would be further along in her career if she were single, but she certainly said that this was a strong possibility.

Patricia participates in Charles's work role and is what we might call a good corporate wife. Her husband's company expects spouses to participate in company social functions, and Patricia does whenever the company includes spouses. She also feels it has been helpful to her husband's career for her to entertain his business associates in their home or some other place, and to accompany him on company family trips and other functions. And, finally, it, too, has been important that Patricia maintain a good rapport with Charles's work associates and their spouses. She participates in these work-related functions on an average of once or twice a month. Again, she attends whenever she is invited. When asked if Charles accompanies her to her business-associated functions her answer was, "He does when he can." We might compare this to her response of "always" when the question was asked in the reverse.

We might conclude from this that Charles is a supportive husband but that his support is appreciated but not as expected. She always attends. When I asked Patricia if her husband's corporation has expectations of her as a wife, she responded affirmatively but feels the definition of the ideal corporate wife is changing. Even in her 5 ½ years of being married to Charles, the expectations have lessened. It was very interesting to me that on the day I was to interview Patricia, we had to reschedule our interview for an earlier hour because Charles had a last-minute business social function to which Patricia was going to accompany him, so she needed time to have her hair done and to go home early to dress for the occasion. Patricia was taking personal leave to leave her office 3 hours early on this particular day to join her husband. Patricia felt very positive about supporting her husband by attending his work-related functions; she tends to be accepting of the fact that he works late hours on a fairly regular basis, and that he travels out of town more frequently than she does.

Patricia mentioned that she had a career change after she and Charles married. At the time of their marriage, they were employed in the same corporation. Because their job areas were rather similar, they sensed that their situation may have been construed within the company as a conflict of interest. So, Patricia moved to another corporation. This also meant a change in job area and type of management. Although Patricia once again feels these were her choices to make and assumes responsibility for these choices, it seemed very apparent to me, although she did not admit to this at first, that Patricia was not as happy in her career change. Patricia, we must again remember, as a single person was employed for 7 years with her former company, which can be viewed as a considerable tenure within a company and within a single job area. She worked very hard to build her career and then after more than 9 years of tenure with this company switched to her present company and a new area of management. My very strong sense was that Patricia was not as happy with her present company or her present position as she had been with her former company. I sensed that her work was not as challenging to her as it used to be, and that she did not feel as "on top of the field" in her new job, although she had been in the new position for 2 years, or as competent in her new field as she had in her former position in which she had invested the first almost 10 years of her corporate career. Patricia did not say that she was unhappy in her work in so many words, but it seemed very definite that although she enjoys her work, she was not enjoying it as much as she once did. Again, Patricia felt this was her choice to make as a liberated, responsible black woman, and because it is her husband who is the major breadwinner, she made the choice in the best interest of her family. She perceives herself as having the freedom to make these choices, and any responsible black woman would choose this option in Patricia's mind. From an objective vantage point one might look at Patricia Bellwood's situation and conclude that she had certainly deferred her own career opportunities in the interest of family. It was required, for whatever reason, aside from the fact that her husband is the major breadwinner, that she subordinate her own career interests, her own career advancement and fulfillment, and sacrifice that which was personally important careerwise, in the interest of her husband's career and in the interest of family concerns.

Patricia reported that her husband, Charles, often shares in household chores. But, of the household chores that Charles performs on a regular basis, the outdoor work (e.g., yard work) was his only assigned task. Charles does perform other domestic duties on an occasional basis, and Charles says that he is very helpful around the house. We can see that Charles's responsibilities—his regular household duties—are rather limited. Patricia's affirmative response to the question of whether or not he performs regular household chores, in light of the fact that his responsibilities are so limited, would indicate her acceptance of traditional male-female roles within the family context and that her expectations of herself are quite high in caring for the homestead, despite the fact that Patricia too has a full-time, highly demanding career.

Patricia confessed that work and family management was sometimes a problem, and she feels guilty about the time that she is away from the children and the time that she neglects household responsibilities. This is something that she wrestles with. But she tries to plan ahead, the kids help her, and she does have a housekeeper who comes into her home one day a week.

In sum, Patricia describes herself as a happy person who is rarely lonely, she is involved in social and civic organizations, attends church on a regular basis, and, in my estimation, is a rather dynamic individual. Patricia Bellwood can be described as a woman of the '90s who, despite some internal struggles over the demands of work and the demands of family and how to juggle the two, is a woman who wants to have it all.

Conclusion

The current state of wives' incorporation has become clouded in part because, as is often the case, attitudes with reference to sex role norms tend to lag behind in the process of change (see Rubin, 1976). Although overt and public behaviors, such as wives filling in as a secretary or acting as a hostess for her husband's business associates, have changed, and certainly there has been a reduction in the frequency of these behaviors, individual attitudes as to definitions of a wife's role have not changed as much as one might guess. To focus on only these outward public types of behaviors without looking at the more private behaviors of wives in the family context, and the social-psychological constructs underlying the phenomenon of wives' corporation, gives the false impression that attitudes toward the wifely role have been totally revolutionized, and that wives' incorporation has ceased to exist.

On the most basic of levels, women (including black women) still feel that the home is primarily their responsibility. They are still the primary caretakers of the children, it is still their role to be emotionally supportive of their husband, and there is still the feeling among corporate families regardless of race that the husband's career comes first—albeit his financial contribution is usually greater—and when necessary wives may have to compromise their own careers and career goals.

The subject of sex role flexibility in black families is an important one in the context of corporate families. Researchers have observed a high degree of sex role flexibility in black families; however, we must also recognize a strong degree of traditionalism or conservativism that simultaneously exists within the black family context. Although there is a tendency to role share when circumstances dictate the necessity, this traditionalism will, in fact, ensue. When, however, absolute necessity or hardship is not operative, behaviors tend to be exhibited more along traditional sex role lines.

In the next chapter, we will look at the issues facing the parents in the sample as they struggle with special child-rearing concerns.

Notes

1. It seems legitimate to assume that in contemporary U.S. society, parenting is no longer considered to be exclusively the mother's job in two-parent households but rather a function that is, at least to some degree, shared in by fathers. Although mothers continue to assume primary responsibility for child care and rearing, fathers' participation has increased in recent years (Fein, 1978).

2. Findings from this research in this area were not significant (in the sense that they were insufficient to be of consequence, versus statistically).

3. Since the late 1960s, women have more visibly fought to gain their own identities independent and distinguishable from their husbands and fathers. Questions have been raised as to the black woman's role in the women's movement. It is the sentiment of many black scholars and writers that black women do not have the same problems or needs as white women and in this respect their role in the women's movement is limited (or at least different) (see Richardson, 1981). Therefore, women's liberation has been considered by some to be a white women's issue and not a black one.

8

Child Rearing

Black Middle-Class Issues and Concerns

My mother said we couldn't invite you.

—White classmate of 7-year-old black corporate youngster

Not many paused to think that the cost of social assimilation might be a loss of identity.

—Morgan, 1985, p. 96

In their struggle for equal rights, blacks in the 1950s and 1960s aimed for equal access to education and employment opportunities, and an end to segregation in housing and public accommodations. To a great extent they have achieved these aims, but with this has come a host of new problems for their children. Although the nature of race relations in many ways has changed, the need to adapt to the conditions of racism persists as a survival tactic. As legal discrimination and overt forms of racism have given way to more covert forms of racism, black parents, who are able to afford their young a childhood that is well protected, fear that their children may not be prepared for the harsher realities that they are likely to confront as adults in a society that today continues to make distinctions between blacks and whites. This chapter will explore this concern.

The Unanticipated Consequences of Integration:
The Renewed Need for Parental Projective Care
in the Socialization of Black Children

The nature of U.S. racism has shifted in the past 30 to 40 years from a period when overt forms of racism including individual racism were pervasive and a persistent cause for daily concern, to a point where the more covert manifestations of racism, which permeate U.S. social institutions, have now become the more prevalent form. We can describe racism as being of two types: individual and institutional, of which the latter tends to be covert and more elusive (Yetman & Steele, 1985).

The children of black corporate managers, by nature of their parents' employment, are middle class. They enjoy the benefits gained by the civil rights movement, and their lives are privileged in ways that surpass the life circumstances of recent previous generations of black middle-class youngsters. They are among the first to be born into and grow up in an "integrated" society.

Blacks who have succeeded climbing the corporate ladder, as a variation of the term "Yuppie," (the acronym for "Young Urban Professional"), have been referred to as "Buppies" (Black Urban Professionals"), or "Bumps" (Black Upwardly Mobile Professionals). Their children, who could be called "Baby Bumps," enjoy the multiple fruits of their parents' achievement. They often live in upper-middle-class and exclusive neighborhoods; they attend private schools, or public schools in affluent communities; they enjoy private lessons and other privileges that their parents can afford. Although all of this translates into greater opportunities for these children than those of other (non-middle-class) black youngsters, it usually also means, in reality, that they are growing up in a predominantly white environment having a predominance of white mainstream experiences in childhood. Although there are obvious educational and economic advantages inherent in the life situations of Baby Bumps, black parents are concerned that there are serious disadvantages for the black child growing up in a mainstream environment and therefore having a predominance of childhood experiences that are race neutral: Black middle-class youngsters may not grow up with a positive sense of self as black, and may not be prepared for adult life in the larger society that is not race neutral, but in which racism persists.

Alternatively, the advantage of children growing up in a black community is that they are more likely to gain a black awareness and self-identity. This is likely to be an expected consequence of the environment. We might say that it is likely to occur almost through osmosis. A drawback to growing up in such an environment is, of course, that it can often, although not always, be equated with poor schools, older housing, and a concern for personal safety.

There are advantages, other than the obvious, however, to growing up in the kind of neighborhoods that Baby Bumps find themselves in—spending one's early years of life free from the concern of physical harm, and growing up with all of the advantages enjoyed by other children of some degree of privilege. These advantages are, however, truly a mixed blessing. The negative side of these advantages is the highly probable fact that black children at some point, usually by their early teens (if not long before), must experience an abrupt departure from their commonality of experience with other nonblack children. As youngsters, they are unable to grasp that when they get older distinctions will be made between them and others. Nor are they as likely as other black children, who grow up in a black environment, to be armed with a strong positive black identity with which to face racism. Thus, they are in for a rude awakening.

The isolated communities that constitute the social world of these corporate black youngsters (school and neighborhood) do not shed light on the realities of what they can expect to encounter in the wider world. This isolated social world gives them no clues as to what lies ahead and therefore cannot and will not prepare these youngsters for their adult (black) experiences (see Banks, 1984). How then are they to be prepared for the future?

If black middle-class youngsters raised in predominantly white communities are to receive the preparation that they need, it must come through interaction with the black community, but, most important, from their parents. (The term "community" as it is used here does not refer to a geographic location or physical place.) An essential element of good parenting for black corporate families in the 1990s is parental projective care that will prepare black youngsters for the realities of racism.

As blacks strove for equality and an end to discrimination in the struggles of the 1950s and 1960s, they saw as the result of their fight better jobs, housing, and the chance for a good education for their children. These were their aims. Blacks were unable to anticipate that one day soon some of them would achieve these things, and were unable to anticipate that there would be associated consequences.

THE BLACK EXPERIENCE:
DIFFERENT AND THE SAME

Many perceive of blacks as a homogeneous group; however, as is the case with any group of its size, there are differences within race among blacks. Ghetto-dwelling blacks or poor blacks are different from middle-class blacks in some very real ways. Lifestyles tend to differ in standard of living and in how members of the two groups spend their leisure time. Access to quality education, educational goals, and the perception of the role of education in one's life may be dissimilar. Patterns of speech, style of dress, and degree of acculturation into the mainstream all may differ between the two groups. Although I would argue that middle-class blacks are "culturally ambidextrous" and fluent in black as well as main-stream culture, their fluency in mainstream culture opens up to them a broader range of experience that in turn affects their goals, preferences, and values. The interactive effect of this cultural duality creates in blacks in the middle class a somewhat different perspective of the world.

There are, of course, commonalities that exist among all blacks. Affluent blacks, although they have achieved upper-middle-class status, still are part of and celebrate black culture. Black Americans of all social strata share a common history, cultural traditions, and cultural values, although the impact and presence of these may be less pervasive in the lives of some blacks than in those of others. Although it is true, however, that a class split exists among blacks and that there is a lack of total identification within race among the various class groups, there is an overriding factor that externally forces racial cohesiveness. Racism, although perhaps in different ways, has an impact on the life chances and experiences of all blacks—regardless of level of income, educational achievement, or job status. One can conclude that there are some differences; but racism, if not shared history and cultural traditions, forces a commonality.

This very factor that forces blacks together, although a negative, could also be their salvation—it will pressure middle-class blacks to address the wider problems that plague the black community. It is they who are best able to bring about change.

The problem is that middle-class status has bought for black children protection, and a "cherished childhood." Their privileged lifestyles in childhood provide these youngsters with an isolated early life experience. Because of this, and because of their own adult experiences, black parents are concerned whether or not their children will be prepared for the realities of racism in the real world.

Some Things We Know About Parenting

Parenting, one of the major life activities that almost all of us engage in, is the one significant area of experience for which we receive virtually no preparation. Schools, the primary socializer of the young second only to family, aim to prepare us for most of our adult roles such as those of citizen and worker; however, they do little to prepare us for roles associated with family living, including the parenting role. The exception to this would be those school districts that have implemented family life education as part of the elementary-secondary curriculum. Parents have few reliable or specific guidelines that they can call on to assist them on the road to successful parenting (see Rossi, 1968). In contemporary U.S. society there persists a social pressure on women to be mothers and for families to raise children (Chodorow, 1978; Hunter College Women's Studies Collective, 1995; Rossi, 1968, 1981; Veevers, 1973).

In addition, the desire to be a good parent is not sufficient to ensure that a particular parent will provide the best possible upbringing for her or his child. Furthermore, we continue to attribute almost full credit (or blame) for the outcome of a child's development to adulthood to its parents, despite refutation by social scientists of the assumptions of parental determinism in child development that were prevalent earlier in this century. These assumptions likened parenting to filling in a blank slate (the child's psychosocial persona), or animal training (see Skolnick & Skolnick, 1986). There are numerous other socializing agents (schools, neighborhood, siblings, peers, media) responsible for individual development to adulthood, and many of these are, to a great extent, beyond the parents' control.

But we do know something about good parenting and what children need from their parents. We do know that there are different needs to be satisfied and different goals to be achieved at the various stages of development, and that children's needs vary with age. Kagan (1976) expressed the importance of the following:

   a. Children perceive that they are valued by their parents and a few other key persons (significant others).
   b. Parents and society should ensure that children have the kinds of experiences that will prepare them for their adult roles, and enable them to meet the problems and challenges they will be faced with in the future.
   c. Children should have role models.
   d. Children should be protected from dissonance in values and experience.

I would like to address the latter points asserted by Kagan, making reference to black children.

Black parents have to work hard to ensure continuity (versus dissonance) between the childhood experience in a protected environment and those experiences to be had in adulthood in the larger environment—in the real world. Gentle and careful exposure to racism, and to black heroes and role models, should be built into the child's early life experience as a continuous part of his or her experience. Exposure to black culture and discussion of racism should not happen via isolated one-time events such as an annual celebration of black history month that then concludes the child's black experience until the next year. Efforts of a continuous nature must be made so that the transition from childhood to adulthood can be as smooth as possible. Already, our society lacks meaningful transitional ceremonies or activities to demarcate and bridge the coming of age (see Benedict, 1934). The transition for protected black corporate children then may be a rough one, unless they receive some preparation from their parents for what lies ahead and for what undoubtedly will be part of their future experience.

Youth Environment		Adult World
Support and security		Racism
Acceptance	_ Child ⟶	Discrimination
Race neutral encounters		Racial distinctions

THE CONTENT OF GOOD BLACK PARENTING

It is difficult to find good instructive literature on parenting in general, and it is almost impossible to find literature on black parenting. Most child-rearing books are geared toward the white middle class. Their patterns and particulars are considered the norm. Furthermore, few books deal with issues of race or race relations.

Often in both professional and lay circles, the discourse on child rearing flows without mention of differences by race. The work of some researchers, however, includes race as a major factor in child rearing, child development, and child supports (Banks, 1984; Bartz & LeVine, 1978; Baumrind, 1972; Clark, 1983; Comer & Poussaint, 1975, 1992; Hale-Benson, 1986; Hopson & Hopson, 1990; Hurd, 1995; Jones, 1989; H. P. McAdoo, 1993; McAdoo & McAdoo, 1985; McLoyd, 1990; Peters, 1981, 1988; Spencer, Brookins, & Allen, 1985, 1991; Washington, 1988; Washington & La Point, 1987; Watson, 1988; Willie, 1989b). Clark (1983), Comer and Poussaint (1975, 1992), and Hopson and Hopson (1990) believe that there are differences in raising a black versus a white child. Their view is that a white-dominated society, that is sometimes hostile to blacks, makes for special problems for both black parents and black children.

They argue that a sense of belonging in society enables parents to accept its values and pass them on to their children. Racism, however, denies blacks the security of belonging—a sense of "oneness" with society. As a corollary to Comer and Poussaint's (1975, 1992) and Hopson and Hopson's (1990) assessments, I would like to suggest that we view this concept of "belonging" in society as something that is experienced by blacks in varying degrees, so that some are likely to have a stronger or weaker sense of belonging than others. Black middle-class corporate families, to a greater extent than others, because of the intimacy with which they share in mainstream culture, "belong." In this sense then, black corporate parents are better able than many other blacks to prepare their children for adulthood in our society.

Black parents, in rearing their children, have to cope with the same concerns that all other parents have in rearing their children. But, in addition, black parents also have to contend with and accommodate the changing faces of racism and the changing social attitudes and values regarding race. As the nature of race relations changes, so, too, must the content of black parenting.

A part of the message that Comer and Poussaint (1975, 1992) were giving black parents in the early to mid-1970s is somewhat different from the concerns about race and racism that parents have today for their children. Although they strongly advocated instilling black pride in children, they were concerned that race would be used as an excuse for such things as poor achievement. Now the concerns for preparing the child for a healthy future would be different—making the child aware of race and racism, rather than being too preoccupied with race and using it as an excuse. This change has come about in response to changes in contemporary race relations.

Race (and racism) causes special problems; black child-rearing practices must take this into account. Although basic child-rearing practices for all U.S. children, given that they occur within the context of U.S. society and U.S. culture, should likely be fundamentally similar. There will, can, and ought to be differences on the basis of different subcultural values and differences in social experience.

> In providing for the psychological well-being of our children, we, as black parents will occasionally need to act in special ways. (Comer & Poussaint, 1975, p. 23)

This is no different from what other groups (e.g., religious ones) have had to do.

What to Do

What specifically can and should black parents do to instill in their children a sense of self as black, and to prepare them for their future and the likelihood that they will experience racism? The following are some suggestions from Comer and Poussaint (1975).

1. Parents should talk to their children about racial injustice. This enables them to recognize racism and to handle it. Research shows that blacks are better at recognizing racism because white children do not get to talk about race and are not educated about the facts. Let me add that black children have an advantage over others—they are socialized to be aware of social injustice. They are able to critique the social order without the

bias of the status quo. This might suggest a tendency to be more humane and thoughtful, a value we would want cultivated in all children regardless of race. This is especially important to develop in black children because they are more frequently the victims of such injustices.

2. Successful blacks should be pointed out to children. They should see parental respect for black art, music, and other aspects of black culture. That blacks are deserving of respect is proven through the actions of significant others (e.g., parents, teachers).

3. It is important for parents to call situations as they are. If it is an act of racism, tell your child so—"you (parent) aid best by helping your adolescent learn to 'see it like it is' " (Comer & Poussaint, 1975, p. 284).

It is also important that parents then follow through on taking any appropriate action that may be called for.

To these suggestions I would like to add that it is of the utmost importance for parents who believe that racism persists to engage in activities that promote change. Their children will gain more of a sense of the reality of things from their parents' criticisms and assertions that racism is alive and well if coupled with constructive action. Parents spending the time and effort to combat racism will instruct young people that it is a serious matter.

PARENTAL PROJECTIVE CARE AND BLACK PARENTS

Demause (1974) expounds eloquently on the psychological principle of parental projective care. With this type of care, the child is used as a vehicle of the content of the parents' projections. That is, it involves the parent "projecting" on the basis of her or his own experience or forethought what the child will face in the future and, in turn, what the child will need as preparation for it. The parent tries to do for the child what he or she thinks is best for the child. It is considered to be good parental care.

Since slavery, black parents have employed the principle of parental projective care in anticipating and preparing their offspring for the racism that they would encounter in the future in adulthood (Toliver, 1982). Just as slave parents knew that the relatively carefree existence that their offspring enjoyed as children would abruptly come to an end with the onset of adulthood in a racist system of slavery, black corporate parents are aware that the carefree existence and race neutrality that their youngsters experience in childhood will change as they move into adulthood and out into a society that continues to be plagued by racism. Although black parents today, as in past eras, try to protect and shelter their offspring in childhood, they also recognize the need to prepare them for the racism that they will experience in adulthood (see Toliver, 1982).

Today, it would seem, the content of good parental projective care for corporate black families would then include

a. Instilling a sense of racial pride
—Identifying black heroes
—Instructing in black culture and history
b. Developing an awareness of their blackness
—Talking about race and race-related issues
—Providing contact with other black youngsters
c. Establishing their sense of self as black
—Maintaining ties with the black community
d. Developing their commitment to combating racial injustice
—Parental example (e.g., letting them see parents do something about racism)

These directives are consistent with the advice of Comer and Poussaint (1975), which we have previously discussed.

SPECIAL BLACK PARENTING CONCERNS

The black middle to upper-middle class has a special set of concerns as parents. This is a powerful added concern to those of parents in general. That is, black parents have a concern for their children's "blackness."

Because racism continues to persist, being black in U.S. society today continues to affect one's life chances, to affect the opportunities available, and to affect one's life experiences. The nature of racism has shifted to manifest itself in more subtle forms; overt expressions of it are less easily found. Thus, black children today do not on a routine basis experience the same social discrimination, sometimes in forms that were life-threatening, as did perhaps their parents or previous generations of blacks when they were children. In fact, many of today's black middle-class youngsters are relatively old (in their teens) before they experience any of these situations. Furthermore, the media, in particular television and music videos, tend to portray black-white relations in a neutral (although unrealistic) light, giving children a sense of equality between the races. Black musicians and white musicians perform together, rock videos portray romantic encounters with and attraction between opposite-race characters. They give one the sense that race is a nonissue in our society. We know the average number of hours that U.S. children spend watching television (Mann, 1982 reports this figure at 6 hours and 44 minutes per day), and research informs us that the media does influence our views of the world.

Black parents, on the other hand, feel quite differently. They are aware of the persistence of racism and they worry about their children. They are concerned that their children, who grow up in predominantly white neighborhoods and attend predominantly white schools, do not as young people get a realistic view of the larger social world. Their youngsters are insulated from the harsher realities of life that they inevitably will encounter in their teen years and as adults. So, although insulated as youngsters, their parents fear what will face them in the future.

RACIAL AWARENESS, SELF-CONCEPT, AND SELF-ESTEEM

Having a good sense of self as a black youngster via having a knowledge of black history and an appreciation for African American culture is important for other reasons in addition to preparing young people for the racism that they are likely to experience later on. The experts (Comer & Poussaint, 1992; Ponterotto & Pedersen, 1993; Spencer et al., 1985, 1991; Spencer, Dobbs, & Swanson, 1988) have found that having a positive sense of one's blackness is important to the development of self-esteem and a positive self-concept. Studies further inform us that academic achievement, so crucial to the future success of black youngsters, is very firmly linked to self-esteem.

Margaret Beale Spencer, over the past more than two decades, has researched the relationship between race awareness and self-concept. In numerous writings, Spencer (see Connell, Spencer, & Aber, 1994; Spencer, 1976, 1988, 1990; Spencer et al., 1985, 1988, 1991; Spencer & Horowitz, 1973; Spencer & Markstrom-Adams, 1990) provides support for the notion that it is imperative for black parents to instill in their children an awareness of their blackness. Parents should inform their children of racism as well as acquaint them with the positive aspects of being black.

Although the literature generally promotes the view that black young-sters must have knowledge of their heritage to develop a positive self-concept and to be prepared for the realities of U.S. racism, I would like to mention the findings of two researchers. In a study of the Atlanta child murders, Spencer et al. (1988) discovered that black parents were not preparing their children for racism. Had children been better pre-pared, Spencer suggests, the event would have been experienced as less of a crisis for the rest of Atlanta's black children. A study by Banks (1984) of middle-class black youngsters being raised in a predominantly white suburban environment found that students who held more pro-black attitudes (perceived as more ethnocentric) scored lower in self-esteem than children who were less pro-black. Banks explained this phenome-non as possibly being the result of those with more pro-black attitudes having experienced discrimination. My feeling is that although they may have been more pro-black and have had more of an appreciation for black culture, their environment could not have prepared them for racism (by virtue of the fact that there is a high degree of egalitarianism among all youngsters in suburbia—this does not begin to change in most instance until the teen years).

This may seem to suggest that the suburban environment is almost an impossible place to prepare youngsters for racism. The few black experiences that these youngsters may have had may seem disconnected with and disassociated from the bulk of their day-to-day experiences. Supplementing the daily routine experiences with "a little blackness" may cause blackness and the relativeness of the black experience in their lives to seem artificial. A black history lesson or experience once or twice a year may not be enough to do it. Coupled with a "cherished childhood" in the mainstream, providing the black experience as a "supplement" may not work. Is providing a suburban experience then, with all the advantages of a good education, safe neighborhood, and expensive home, really the best experience a parent can provide for his or her children? And, at what cost? It may not be as good as we think. We must at least recognize that there is a downside.

Evidence That Parental Fears
Are Well-Founded

There is evidence that black parents' fears for their children are well-founded. One can point to the numerous recent racially motivated uprisings on predominantly white college campuses being experienced by college young people today. Displays of antiblack sentiment have recently occurred in the South as well as in the "liberal northeast" and in California—ranging from name calling to cross burnings to fistfights to brutal beatings to homicide. Many black students say they have been taken by surprise, and social scientists claim that many are unprepared for these attacks. These are examples of some of the incidents of racism that black middle-class parents fear their children are unprepared for.

At a recent Discrimination Forum at a New York City college that was motivated by racist acts perpetrated against a black faculty member, students expressed shock that this kind of thing (writing "nigger" across the professor's office door, and assaulting him with racist graffiti around the urban campus) could happen at their school on the eve of the 21st century. No one quite knew what to do.

Psychologist Ogretta McNeil, professor at the small Worcester, Massachusetts College of the Holy Cross, worries about black youth. An article in the *Black Collegian* (Turner, 1985) states that McNeil "cautions that a campus with a predominately white student body is not the place for blacks who are uncertain about who they are to find out" (p. 24).

Findings

I pursued the subject of race relations with a group of 21 preparatory school youngsters, 19 of whom were children of black and other minority corporate managers. The fathers of the other two children were physicians, one mother a nurse, and the other a school guidance counselor. Although they are not children of corporate managers, their experiences are appropriate to include in this discussion because their lifestyles are similar by virtue of their upper-middle-class status. It becomes relevant to point out that the parental concern for black corporate children is much the same concern that is held by other black middle-class parents for their children, whose life situations are similar because of their class status. Thus, the phenomenon is largely an artifact of social class affected by parents' corporate managerial employment status and income.

In speaking of prejudice, discrimination, and stereotypes with these children, I was struck by the separation and distinction made by many of the black (and Hispanic) "preppies" between themselves and blacks in general, or "the blacks," as they referred to them. When asked for stereotypes about blacks, they talked about blacks as "they" and "them."

When it was explained to the group that stereotypes are based on false assumptions, and, occasionally, on some small kernel of truth, they challenged with statements such as "Well, blacks *do* steal . . . and hang out in gangs . . . and carry 'ghetto blasters' " (large portable radios).

Two of the main points to be concluded from the group session are the following:

1. These black and minority youngsters do not identify with the black community.
2. These youngsters have "bought" a negative image of blacks, such as that presented by the media, which more often shows blacks in the news, being arrested for various types of crime, rather than in any kind of positive light.

These young people seemed to believe that there are two kinds of children: minorities and preppies—and they (blacks) were preppies, just like the other (white) kids who sit beside them in their classrooms. For these youngsters (from their view), class is a more salient divider of people or social groups. They would support William J. Wilson's (1978a) thesis of class over race. They also very firmly identified black (or minority) with lower class, something that they very definitely were not. Although this sample of preppies is small, their views regarding race were consistent with those of other children of corporate managers in the sample.

I was struck by the way in which one girl, whom we will call Lisa, talked in a very patronizing way about other blacks who were not "Highlands kids" (the upper-middle-class neighborhood that she lives in that is adjacent to a low-income area with a fairly large minority population) like she was. She explained to us the differences in their clothing—Highlands kids wear Benetton, blacks wear Nike sneakers and Sergio Valente clothing—differences in their speech, and so on. She said that she and her mother used to try to "educate" the lower-class black kids by taking them to cultural and activities (mainstream culture, not black) such as museum exhibits and plays. But she said the other kids "just couldn't absorb it all. They couldn't really take advantage of it." So, she and her mother had given up. No more "cultural enrichment excursions" for the blacks from the nearby area.

Lisa also talked about a former friend whom she described as "really stupid" because she passed up an opportunity to go to private parochial school in favor of the local public school, because she wanted to be with her friends. Lisa had no understanding or tolerance for the former friend—no understanding for the security of being in a familiar environment with friends, the power of peer pressure, perhaps the possible lack of savvy that her friend's mother had about which education would be best for the child, or other possible explanations for the choice of schools. The friend was simply written off, without compassion, as "stupid."

Lisa told the group that the black kids from the other neighborhood said she was "stuck up" and that she was turning her back on being black. She says that she is not stuck up and that she is proud of being black— surprising in light of how she talked and her attitude toward blacks who are not like her. But, it seemed likely that this young woman should feel no responsibility to those in her community (black) when she reached adulthood. She had already written them off. Some youngsters never go so far as to make the attempt, although perhaps paternalistic, to "enlighten" others of their race who are less fortunate. It is not their problem, it has nothing to do with them. It was never their concern and it never will be.

They also seemed, in some small way, embarrassed about blacks. Lauren, another young black girl, talked about blacks in an objectified fashion, as a group very much apart from herself and from those with whom she identifies. When she described blacks as "people who play loud music and carry big radios," someone in the room chided her, saying that they had noticed her radio (of course she did not have one). In response she frowned, mumbled a few words, and became defensive in her posture and body language. I think that she was surprised to have the stereotype projected back at her and embarrassed by it. Very vocal up to this point in our group discussion, she became reticent for the remainder of the session. (I spoke privately with Lauren about her feelings after the group session.)

ON RACISM

Many of the corporate families in this study pointed to recent incidents of racism that their children had experienced. Included are the testimonies of respondent members of three such families. Although the teenage children were more likely to be faced with discriminatory situations, incidents of young children (aged 5 and 6 years) experiencing racism were also reported. The first of the following is an account of one mother and her young child's experience, the second account is a teenager's, the third is of a family with three children of varying ages. They speak of the youngsters' feelings of hurt, shock, anger, and lack of fairness.

* * * * *

Mrs. Robinson, a suburban mother whom I interviewed, spent a great deal of time investigating the private schools in her area to find the one that would offer the best all-around educational opportunity for her children. At first, she was quite satisfied with the school she had chosen and delighted with her children's progress there. But after a couple of racial incidents experienced by her second grader, her oldest child, she became disheartened and angry. The final incident proved to be too hurtful.

One of little Nicole's classmates had a big birthday celebration, complete with gifts of a stuffed animal (valued at about $50.00) for each child, and a performance by a professional marionette company. All of the children in the second-grade class talked on and on about the good time had at the party on the next class day. That is, all but Nicole, who was not invited. Nicole, with hurt feelings and a tear in her eye, asked why she had not been invited. The birthday girl told her, "My mother said we couldn't invite you." Nicole is the only black youngster in her class.

Mrs. Robinson told of her frustration and hurt in trying to explain and soothe the situation for her daughter, who came home that day in tears. "The poor baby was so upset and confused; she couldn't understand why her little friend didn't like her and kept asking, "Why doesn't she like me?" This mother did not expect that her children would experience discrimination so early in life. It was this incident that prompted Mrs. Robinson to enroll her children at another school.

* * * * *

Corporate manager Clifford Jones shares his story. Cliff Jones, from a grassroots family background, had worked his way up to a prestigious upper-middle-management position in corporate America. He told me of an experience had by his teenage son. The boy was raised in a predominantly upper-middle-class community and had less frequent contact with other black youngsters than his father would have cared for.

Michael, aged 16, was a fine student and had always excelled in ath-
letics. Enrolled in one of the nation's top northeastern prep schools, his
grades were good and he was a star campus athlete. He was popular and
generally well liked.

Ever since he was old enough to recall, Michael's father has told him
that he should be proud of his blackness, and never to let anyone mistreat
him because of it. Mr. Jones in particular instilled the lesson that, "If
anyone ever calls you nigger, you make sure that he's on the ground
before he can call you that twice." Michael, who had had few personal
exposures to racial injustice, was not quite sure that he understood his
father's concern, or why he should hit someone for using that word.

One day, after a game of intramural football, the call of a certain play
evoked a confrontation between Michael and his rival, one of the opposing team players. Some words were exchanged. The rival called
Michael a nigger. Michael, remembering his father's words, decked the
youth with one solid punch.

The "fight" was reported to the assistant headmaster, who called to
see Michael immediately and demanded that he explain his behavior.
The youngster explained what had happened and also told of his father's
instructions. The assistant headmaster telephoned Michael's father and
said that violence was not condoned at their institution and that Mr.
Jones would have to rescind his teachings or his son would be expelled.
Mr. Jones responded that if the school could promise that Michael
would never again be called that name he would promise that Michael
would never strike another student. When the headmaster got wind of
the incident, a formal letter of apology was sent to Michael's parents
and a workshop on racial awareness was given for the full student body.
Michael, surprised by the incident, began to understand his father's
fears.

* * * * * *

Ted Campbell shares a disheartening tale of discrimination. Campbell, a middle-aged corporate manager and father of three children, told
me that he was glad when he and his family had an experience of racial
discrimination. The occurrence took place while the family was traveling
home from visiting relatives in the South. Although the event took
Campbell by surprise, his children were amazed with disbelief.

After driving all day en route back to their New York-area home, the
Campbells decided to stay the night in a small town in Maryland, just

outside of Washington, D.C. They came to a motel whose vacancy sign was lit and the Campbells went in to register. They were told by the person at the desk that there were no vacancies. When Campbell queried about the sign, he was told that someone had forgotten to turn on the "No Vacancy" sign. The sign was then switched on. The family turned away and fortunately found a motel just a short way down the road where they were able to rent rooms for the night.

After taking their bags out of the car and into their rooms, the kids talked their dad into taking them back down the road to a Dairy Queen they had spotted across the highway from the first motel. They piled back into the car in quest of their midnight snack. As they pulled into the Dairy Queen, they noticed that the vacancy sign at the motel was once again lit. As the kids were getting their ice cream, they saw a white family pull into the motel and enter the office. They then left the office, got their luggage from their car, and took it inside one of the motel rooms, obviously to bed down for the night.

The Campbell children thought what they had seen was incredible. They were up in arms with questions and protests. "That isn't fair," exclaimed Campbell's daughter.

To Campbell, who says that his kids think of the civil rights movement as part of a long past era, this was an eye-opening experience for his children to have. He saw it as their introduction to the real world. The family then retired to their motel, where the father tried to explain to his children what had happened and to put the event into the proper context for them.

The event enabled Campbell to use a concrete example based on their own experience to talk to his children about racism and discrimination and provided an opportunity for them to discuss in a constructive fashion how to deal with racism.

* * * * *

Most of the parents in the sample were generally happy about the kinds of opportunities that they could provide for their kids. But these opportunities did not come without fears. The reality of providing youngsters with a wholesome sense of self as black in the context of these privileged environments remains a challenge. It is possible, but it is not easy.

Discussion

ASSIMILATION MODELS AND THE
CONTINUING SIGNIFICANCE OF RACE

A seemingly relevant perspective to consider in the context of analyzing black middle-class parents' concerns for their children based on this research would be that of assimilation. Essentially, the experience of black upper-middle-class corporate youngsters and parental concerns therein is one of acculturation. Let us consider briefly the situation of black corporate families, particularly the children, in the context of assimilation theories and the impediments of their full assimilation.

Gordon (1964) indicates that attempts at creating theoretical models to address the assimilation process and to ease the adjustment of racially and culturally different people into the U.S. mainstream are all but lacking completely. Relatively little attention has been given to this endeavor. Three primary schools of thought have developed historically in connection with the phenomenon of assimilation: (a) Anglo conformity, (b) melting pot, and (c) cultural pluralism.

In brief, the first view espouses complete abandonment of the immigrant culture and total acceptance of the values of the new Anglo American culture. The second view envisioned a blending of the indigenous and immigrants, biologically and culturally. In the third view, the preservation of the immigrant cultures was advocated. Subcultural integrity would be maintained while actively participating in the social, political, and economic life of U.S. society (see Gordon, 1964). This third view was a later development of the 20th century. It is, of course, the first of these views, Anglo conformity, that most accurately characterized the reality of assimilation for racial and ethnic minorities in the United States in the 20th century. Although the rise of assimilation theories was inspired by the immigration of culturally dissimilar, non-Anglo-Saxon peoples from Eastern Europe and Asia, as well as the enfranchisement of black slaves and their lack of "fit" within the Anglo American culture, it was not expected that blacks would ever be candidates for assimilation into U.S. society in the early days in this country (Gordon, 1964).

The debate whether or not affirmative action programs for black Americans are necessary or justified has ensued for more than three decades. Some argue that the black experience was not unique, and therefore no special programs are required. Of those who hold this view, there are two schools of thought. There is the "bootstraps" notion, which claims that those who work hard can lift themselves up and improve their lot. The other notion is that blacks are the "last of the immigrants," based on their late migration to the nation's urban centers. Accordingly, it is expected that blacks will undergo the same assimilation/ acculturation experiences of previous immigrant groups. All immigrants had a hard time at first. Blacks are no exception. Black assimilation from both the bootstraps and the last-of-the-immigrants points of view should be only a matter of time and hard work. Affirmative action programs are unwarranted.

On the other side of the debate, scholars including Blauner (1972), Gordon (1964), and Hershberg, Burstein, Ericksen, Greenberg, and Yancey (1979) argue that assimilation models do not work for blacks largely due to racial discrimination. The black parents in my sample, on the basis of their own personal experiences past and present, agree with them.

Traditional models have viewed assimilation as a three-stage or three-generation process, with each successive generation being more highly assimilated than the last. Intergenerational conflict has often been characteristic of families whose members are engaged in different stages of the process. The pushes and pulls of holding on to the subgroup culture while acculturating into the mainstream make for friction across generations.

Is black parental concern for their children's "blackness" merely the same kind of intergenerational concern or conflict that ensues in white ethnic families whose children have progressed to a subsequent stage of the assimilation process? Studies of Italian Americans (Gambino, 1974), for example, speak to the tension that ensues between first- and third-generation Italian Americans, with the first generation criticizing the third as it begins to pull away from traditional ethnic cultural values and behaviors and becomes more "Americanized," and the third generation not understanding the need of the first to hold on to the old. But, is this an assimilation issue or problem in the case of blacks, and, if so, in what ways? If the age cohort of young children of black corporate managers can be seen as the third generation, can focus on parental concerns and holding on to the culture be viewed as the intergenerational concern that is typical in the model?

Hershberg et al. (1979), in focusing on the assimilation process of various groups, including blacks, in three time periods in Philadelphia, argue that assimilation is not an appropriate model for viewing and understanding the experience of blacks in the United States. Furthermore, they argue that the impediments to black assimilation rest in limited ecological and opportunity structures (availability of housing, economic conditions, needs of the labor force for skilled versus unskilled workers, and so on), but also, in large part to acute racial discrimination—discrimination that denies blacks access to opportunity. In concurrence, I contend that the traditional models alone are not adequate for viewing the black experience.

Although Hershberg et al. (1979) argue that a major impediment to black upward mobility is related to ecological conditions or structures, it is important to point out that race, unlike ethnicity for European immigrant groups, serves as a tenacious barrier to total black assimilation. The fact that those blacks for whom the opportunity structures were favorable and who have achieved a modicum of success continue to face barriers by way of discrimination is a testament to the significance of race as a factor that distinguishes the experience of blacks versus white ethnics in their struggles toward upward mobility and "fit" in U.S. society.

Charles Willie (1978, 1979, 1989a), the leading opponent of the class over race as greater determinant of the life chances of blacks controversy, as previously discussed in Chapter 1, feels that race and racial discrimination are still powerful factors. Race and racial discrimination, in a multiplicity of ways, negatively affect black lives and black well-being, even across class lines to include the most affluent and accomplished. Willie focuses on issues such as black-white differences in income even when controlling for education, and access to opportunity, contending that, "In general, the proportion of high-income blacks is far less than what it would be if there was no racial discrimination" (Willie, 1978). The basis of his argument does not end with demographic differentials and incongruous socioeconomic factors. It goes on to point to the effect of race on even another level.

Willie (1978, 1979, 1989a, 1989b) posits that the significance of race has increased especially for the middle and upper classes. He focuses on this notion of the heightened significance of race by highlighting the intense degree of consciousness about one's racial identity that society forces on those blacks who are achievers in areas where black achievement is a relatively new and/or limited phenomenon. Willie reports that middle-class black families attest that race can be a "consuming experience" for those blacks who live and work in integrated settings where one must constantly prove oneself, where one is made to feel conspicuous because of one's racial identity, and where one is always susceptible to being used as a token.

Although my interviews with black corporate managers and their spouses provide strong support for Willie's (1978, 1979, 1989a, 1989b) arguments, William J. Wilson's (1978a) thesis, which posits class over race as a determinant of black success, cannot be ignored. The children of these managers, who are middle class, are much more likely to fare better than working-class or poor black ghetto children and have a good chance for a successful future. Of course, having the economic resources of good schools, special educational helps, broad exposures, educated parents, and so forth are a help and make a difference. But, this does not preclude the fact that racism will and is likely to impede their progress toward their goals, and is an inescapable negative that they will experience in the broader world. Blacks still, even in the middle class and with college degrees, do not have equal earning power with whites of similar educational background or equal job status. Recent evidence provided by the National Research Council (Jaynes & Williams, 1989) continues to support this difference in the strength of the correlation between education and income by race. It was also the view of the managers in this sample that this difference holds true in the corporate world. Managers generally felt that they were better educated and more experienced than their white counterparts in their companies.

Conclusion

It can be argued convincingly that black middle-class youngsters today have assimilated culturally and socially to a greater extent than their parents. This is true even for those parents who, too, were middle class in their youth. Evidences of this include primary friendships and association with whites, and participation in mainstream popular culture such as having an appreciation for white popular music, the presence of posters of white rock video stars on black teenagers' bedroom walls, and sporting certain hair and clothing fashions. But, can we argue that assimilation has been total? And can we ensure that black young people, once they have reached adulthood and have entered the real world, will experience no more racism and discrimination than third-generation offspring of white immigrants? Of course not! The evidence suggests otherwise.

Parental fears are likely to be well-founded in that parents recognize that race is still significant in determining one's life chances and experiences in this society. Willie's (1978) view of the "inclining" significance of race is supported by the black families who are the subjects of this research. To suggest that the third generation of black youngsters ("Baby Bumps") is safe from racism would require operating on the premise that race is no longer a salient factor. But black corporate parents feel and know that it is. Furthermore, because of their sheltered and protected childhood existence, black corporate youngsters may lack preparation for the real world in their teenage years and adulthood in a most critical area that still today includes racism. And, thus the fears.

In this chapter, we have focused on black parents' concern that their youngsters lack awareness of and appreciation for the full fact of their difference. The next chapter focuses on black managers' own inescapable awareness of being different in the corporate environment. They are outsiders in the mainstream. Let us turn our attention to the experience of being a race-marginal individual in corporate America.

9

Inside-Outside

Themes of Marginality

Sometimes I walk into a meeting with people who are junior to me in the company and I'm not sure if they are responding to me as they do because I'm black, because of my position, or both.

—William Murray, black male manager

This chapter explores the concept of marginality theoretically and experientially. Its aims are to speak to the difficulties and morass of marginality, and to build a positive appreciation for the uniquely valuable status of marginality. The findings suggest that although black corporate managers struggle through the quandaries of marginal status, upwardly mobile black families also can and do enjoy the benefits of their success in corporate America, and at the same time appreciate and enjoy their African American culture. The pains of the marginal experience endured by these managers help to reap the positives of marginality for them, their wives, and especially for their children—the best of both worlds.

Definitions and Perspectives, Dilemmas of Marginality

Although the concept of marginality has been recognized by early sociologists such as Simmel (1955), it was most likely in the work of

Park (1928) that the term was coined and a name given to the phenomenon. Park suggested that there are two general root causes of marginality. The first of these has to do with migration and the introduction of the immigrant to foreign shores—the immigrant who experiences both an enthusiasm or hunger for the new life which he or she is not yet fully a part of, and a homesickness for the comfort and security of the old ways. The second conception deals with what Park refers to as the cultural hybrid. He defines marginality in this context as

> a man living and sharing intimately in the cultural life and traditions of two distinct peoples; never quite willing to break, even if he were permitted to do so, with his past and his traditions, and not quite accepted, because of racial prejudice, in the new society in which he now sought to find a place. (p. 892)

It is this concept of marginality that is important to us here.

Moving from the definitional bases of Park (1928), with particular emphasis on the cultural hybrid definition of marginality, Hughes (1949) looks at marginality from the perspective of status and its accompanying social roles. He focuses on blacks as well as women in exemplifying various aspects of marginality. Hughes elaborates that certain groups of people, such as blacks or women, are associated with a particular status and roles in society. Confusion happens when a member of a group takes on a status and role that is not usually associated with a member of his or her group (in this case, race or sex). This is a source of confusion for both ego (the actor) and the others with whom ego interacts.

Consider the case of a black man occupying the status of a top line manager. Does one treat him as a black, or as a manager? Thus, the confusion.

One black male manager, when I asked if he feels he is treated differently in the work environment because he is black, responded as follows:

> Although I'd have to say yes, I must admit that at times it's hard to tell. Sometimes I walk into a meeting with people who are junior to me in the company and I'm not sure if they are responding to me as they do because I'm black, because of my position, or both.

Similarly, the black manager, in determining his or her own courses of action and behaviors, might be faced with the dilemma of having to decide in what ways and in what instances or situations he or she should participate in the organization as a black, or as a manager. The dilemma is likely to be compounded by gender for the female manager—does she participate as a female, a black, a manager, or in some other way stemming from the interaction of these statuses? So long as such dilemmas exist in the mind of the marginal person (in this case, the black manager) or for those with whom he interacts, so, too, persists marginality.

We must note that the statuses and respective social roles associated with social groups other than the dominant group, such as the status of blacks, are less than that afforded to white males, the dominant group in this country, and their respective social roles. Inherent in a status-linked approach to marginality is the problem that people tend to have abilities that exceed and surpass the boundaries of that which their status may allow. Hughes alluded to this notion in his 1949 article. Therefore it is possible to have blacks and women who can be competent doctors, lawyers, congresspersons, mayors, and corporate managers. We do find blacks in each of these roles in contemporary U.S. society. When we talk about blacks and women taking on roles that are considered nontraditional for their group, we are also speaking about their assuming roles that have a higher status attached to them than the roles that are usually associated (stereotypically) with members of these groups.

There are several points that are important to raise pertaining to the circumstances of female and minority upwardly mobile marginal individuals. First of all, these marginal individuals tend to be found in relatively small numbers, in isolated instances, in the niches of the status hierarchies that are not typically their own. Thus, their presence becomes conspicuous. We might also mention that as one moves higher up the status ladder, marginality, in a sense, gets worse because one encounters fewer of his or her race cohort and becomes even more of an exception to the rule.

Thus:

— the problems of tokenism are enhanced;
— the possibilities for fellowship with same race-sex peers are even more limited; and
— a distance is created between self and other members of one's race or sex within the organization in job status differentials, and contact is decreased.

THE POSITIVE ASPECTS OF MARGINALITY

In recent years, several works have been published that focus on blacks in business (America, 1978; Boyd, 1991; Collins, 1979; Davis & Watson, 1982; Dickens & Dickens, 1982; Epstein, 1973; Fernandez, 1975, 1981; Hopkins, 1987; Irons & Moore, 1985; Jones, 1986; Leggon, 1980; Nixon, 1985a, 1985b, 1985c). They focus on a number of topics and issues including the dilemmas and experiences both positive and negative of upwardly mobile African Americans in the professional and managerial workplace.

Traditionally, however, the focus in the literature on blacks as marginal employees in the business world has frequently been associated with the negative aspects of marginality and tokenism. This obscures the benefits of dual identity. Frazier (1957), Kardiner and Ovesey (1949), Redding (1951), and others address the dilemmas of being an outsider generally in the white world, whereas Kanter (1977) and Fernandez (1981) address them specifically in the context of the corporate world. The former even argue that blacks suffer psychologically from identity confusion, suggesting that racial identity poses a psychological burden for blacks in America. Frazier (1957), in *Black Bourgeoisie,* states that the problem increases for blacks who have climbed the social-status ladder by being confused about who they are, and thus race provides another special kind of burden. Such black elites, in Frazier's view, because their socioeconomic status has distanced them from the masses of black people and because the color of their skin separates them from the mainstream of society, are neither black nor white. The negative aspects of a dual identity and the assumed ensuing problems have been often spoken of in the literature. The positive aspects of a dual identity have not been emphasized, however, or the strengths associated therein, or the strengths associated with having membership in two worlds. Even if full membership in one of these worlds (the white world) is in several ways restricted, I would like to suggest that having two communities, instead of only one, to draw resources from can certainly suggest advantage in the situation of the marginal person—for example, in the case of the black corporate manager. A focus on the concept of marginality and women can also be found in the literature (see Githens & Prestage, 1977). In their case as well, we could make similar arguments for the advantages of dual memberships.

Let us refer once again to the work of Park (1928). Although Park examines the psychological conflict aspect of marginality, he also recognizes the societal benefits of the condition, at least in a limited way, and a certain advantage of the marginal person. He speaks of marginality as the situation or necessary condition that makes civilization possible. The marginal individual is ripe for the civilization process to move ahead. Although he suggests that marginality produces an "unstable character," he also asserts that

> it is in the mind of the marginal man that the conflicting cultures meet and fuse. It is, therefore, in the mind of the marginal man that the process of civilization is visibly going on, and it is in the mind of the marginal man that the process of civilization may best be studied. (p. 881)

Park (1928) views the marginal person as a sort of cosmopolitan, able to look at the world into which he or she was born with a certain degree of detachment. He or she is free and not bound by local particulars. His or her behavior is not constricted by the local conventions. The freedom of the marginal person that Park suggests and the ability to view one's own subcultural world of origin with a certain degree of sober objectivity speaks to, at least on a philosophical level, the positive potential and advantages within the marginal condition.

Different Is Positive: These Findings

I would like to add to the discussion of status marginality by elaborating on the notion that marginals are an elite group, and on the inherent positiveness of elite status. Part of the positive side of marginality rests in having this elite status, but this is only one of the aspects of its positiveness—the others being (a) having the opportunity to draw from the best of two worlds, and (b) being part of a subcultural group from which one can draw strength.

Blacks today, who have economically assimilated into the mainstream, can and do enjoy many aspects of middle-class U.S. culture. Black corporate managers are part of this group. Managers and their spouses are able to enjoy the theater and museums. They spend their leisure time skiing and playing tennis. They send their children for dance and music lessons and gymnastic instruction. They enjoy gourmet ice cream and dining in fine restaurants. In short, they are Americans in much of what they do, value, and enjoy.

But, black corporate families also have another milieu in which they live. They are active in black civic and social organizations. They participate in black community functions and are members of the black church. They enjoy black popular music, eat traditional black ethnic food dishes, and attest to appreciating certain special qualities of their same-race friendships. They truly enjoy the best of both worlds.

The subcultural membership often serves as a haven and a source of strength for black managers and their families. The subculture contains its own avenues for making new friendships, for obtaining social recognition and achievement (important because the white world often has limited avenues for blacks to attain these things), and for gaining a sense of belonging/community. These positive aspects of dual membership, highly operative in the experience of the black corporate managers and their families in this study, need to be recognized.

An important antecedent factor in the rise to elite status of these individuals as black people in the corporate managerial ranks is that many of them were superstars in some way before entering the corporate world. For many of the respondents in this research, this status of marginality was theirs to claim long before they joined the ranks of corporate management. In most instances, the family of origin was key as a motivating and supportive factor in launching them into marginal status. Families supported these managers as youngsters by nurturing them, building their self-esteem, and encouraging them in their studies. Many of these managers were exceptional students, National Merit Scholars, and students in Ivy League undergraduate colleges and business schools. Because most of the black managers interviewed were from working-class backgrounds, many of them had to be bright enough to win scholarships to attend college. This was especially true of the older cohort of managers who entered college prior to the existence of affirmative action admissions policies. Some are graduates of Harvard, Princeton, Stanford, and other prestigious institutions. Similar to the findings of Epstein's (1973) study of successful black females, a significant number of the managers I interviewed, beginning in their youth, saw themselves as different, as special, as destined for success. Their families often were instrumental in fostering this success as they grew up. Among these managers are George Emerson, Henry Daniels, Carl Burton, Jennifer Hunter, Walter Tatum, Charles Roland, Patricia Bellwood, and Nathan Brown. The profile of Nathan Brown is expanded.

George Emerson (age 37)

From a working-class rather than middle-class family background, because of his birth order (youngest of the children), his family, including siblings, saw to it that he had opportunities that the others did not. This family focus on George's achievement made him feel that he would succeed and have a bright future. "A lot was expected of me . . . but I expected a lot of myself."

Henry Daniels (age 46)

Born in a poor eastern industrial town, Henry attributes his greater level of success compared with that of his childhood peers to his self-motivation and drive.

"I was different from the other kids in that I had the drive to get ahead." He describes himself as an honor student and talks of his grand-mother's praise for his intellectual acumen.

Carl Burton (age 36)

The son of a laborer, Carl "wanted to earn money and to be successful from as far back as I can remember." He describes himself as an exceptional student in high school and finished college with a grade point average of 3.4.

Jennifer Hunter (age 36)

Raised in a single-parent household, she was forced to be independent and a self-starter. Her mother's experience of going back to school for her degree in nursing after the death of Jennifer's father motivated Jennifer to strive for success in her own future.

"I've always known that I would be a career woman. I've always aimed high."

Walter Tatum (age 48)

Walter always applied himself in his studies and believed that with hard work and faith in God he could make something of his life.

Charles Roland (age 31)

The son of a janitor and a cleaning woman, his mother pushed him from early childhood to achieve. He knew that he wanted a more financially comfortable life than his parents were able to have.

Patricia Bellwood (age 35)

"I was a good student and always loved school."

Although all of her siblings were good students, Patricia's grades were better. Her grades were among the highest in her classes in almost all of her subjects.

A more detailed profile of Nathan Brown follows. He is one among many managers who showed signs of exceptional aptitude and "specialness" from an early age. His profile is evidence of significant career success, the importance of black family and black community support, the perception that blacks are afforded different treatment in the corporate world, that black managers experience the problems of tokenism, that affirmative action is still necessary and important to combat racism, and that belonging to a subculture is more an added source of strength and joy rather than a burden.

Nathan Brown (age 36)

Brown is a manager employed with his company for 13 years. His present company is his first and only employer since completing his education. He has been promoted nine times during his tenure there. He is married and has two children. Nathan describes himself as an exceptional student. He was valedictorian of his high school class and a National Merit Scholarship winner. He went on to complete his B.S. and has an MBA from an Ivy League university. He is hardworking and self-motivated. When asked what he attributes his success to, he identifies his strong work ethic, feels that he is self-motivated, but stresses the importance of the strong family support that he received from the time he was a child and continues to receive. His wife is a college graduate, works 30 hours per week, and cares for their young daughters. In talking to others in Brown's company, he is well respected by his black as well as his white peers. His annual salary exclusive of bonuses and additional compensation is a hefty six figures. He was recruited to the company out of business school and was attracted to the company because it was young and aggressive, and he saw it as a place that held opportunity for someone such as himself. On joining the company, he immediately became an active member of the company's minority caucus. He describes his participation in the caucus within the company as being instrumental to and supportive of his career.

In his leisure time, Nathan enjoys golfing, fishing, and traveling. He and his family have vacationed in such places as Jamaica, the Bahamas, and spots on the California coast. His extra income goes toward investments, vacations, and recreational activities.

When asked if racism still exists in the corporate world, he appears to be surprised that one would even have to ask the question. He answers with a definitive "yes." This assessment comes from a man who, as an individual, has achieved much moving up through the corporate ranks. He thinks that affirmative action programs are very important. He feels very strongly about them, and also feels that blacks would not have been able to achieve the gains they have without the assistance of government programs and corporate policies that involved the active recruitment of blacks.

In Brown's estimation, he is treated differently from others in the corporation because he is black. He is treated differently by peers, superiors, and subordinants as well. He emphatically states that he would be further along in his career if he were white, and feels that racism still exists in the corporate world. Blacks, in Brown's view, are still not fully integrated into the corporate setting because of the biases that are still held by many whites in the corporate world. These are whites who are not accustomed to interacting with blacks so closely, and so racist attitudes still exist. Brown is very much at ease in dealing with his coworkers, both black and white, and, again, commands a great deal of respect from both groups. In his free time, however, Brown prefers to have some distance from the corporate environment, and prefers to "let down his corporate hair" in the company of blacks. Of his socializing in his free time, 90% is with blacks, and his five closest friends are blacks. He is active in black civic and social organizations, and finds them an important source of new friendships. When asked why he prefers to socialize with blacks, he says that it is not always, but most often, his preference because with blacks he shares common experiences—they have a common ground from which they can interrelate juggling family and job responsibilities, managing the pressures of racism, and being black in the predominantly white corporate environment. Brown feels the black world is small from the standpoint that few blacks are highly educated. It is often possible when you make new black acquaintances that you know someone that they know, or you know their family, or schoolmates. There is some connection. He sees himself as being part of a black social network and finds his activity in such networks both enjoyable and energizing.

But, most important, Brown points to the role that his family of origin has played throughout his life, from his childhood to the present. He feels he can count on his family for support and understanding. He says this not only of his parents but of his siblings as well. He communicates often with his family and visits them twice monthly despite the fact that their places of residence are 60 miles apart. Brown receives emotional and spiritual support from his family as well as support in the form of child care. The help and support that he receives from his family are extremely important in his life—not so much the material forms of support but the emotional and psychological support that he receives and this is, in his word, invaluable. This network of support is reciprocal. Family definitely outranks friends, coworkers, and community in the level of support it provides.

Nathan describes himself as a religious person who attended church on a regular basis as a child and continues to do so today on a fairly frequent basis. He credits his wife for being highly understanding of the demands of his job and for being most supportive. She generally understands the frustrations of his work, or at least thinks she does, and is available to provide a listening ear or to provide a shoulder to lean on. Overall, she is supportive of his career and although she may complain, but infrequently, about the time that he spends away from the family because of long work hours, he feels that the job puts a lot less stress on his marriage than it could, compared with the complaints that his white coworkers hear from their wives. She sometimes expresses the wish that he had more time with his family but is always responsive to his needs, always there for him, and always willing to pitch in and cover for him in assuming his domestic responsibilities. All in all, he feels that his wife's attitude is, "We're in this together," and that she is most often enthusiastic about sharing the pressures and demands of his job. There is, as he puts it, a common ground or a common bond that he and his wife and children and also his extended family share. They push together, they plug together, they fight together, but there are times when it is difficult.

Tokenism is something that Brown experiences on two levels, the first being that he is one of very few blacks who have achieved his level of success within his company. On another level, he feels his participation, his performance, and his presence stand out more. In his terms, he suffers from the experience of "high optics" because he is black. He is most noticeable. He states that there is not a lot of opportunity to perform in other than a quality manner. Despite having high visibility and never having a chance to put his head on the desk so to speak, Brown has given a quality performance and has succeeded despite the obstacles of tokenism. To fuel up for the stresses of being black in corporate employ, which affords him and his family a more than comfortable lifestyle, Nathan Brown draws strength and support from his family and friends, both of whom he values and enjoys immensely, and from other blacks in the workplace.

Although Nathan enjoys the theater, a good book, Vivaldi, and a full-bodied cabernet, he also enjoys the sounds of Lionel Richie and Toni Braxton, African art, and cooking some traditional black southern dishes. So we see there are benefits in being culturally "bilingual," because Nathan Brown truly enjoys the best of both worlds.

Discussion and Conclusion

We must recognize that the very term *marginality* is Anglocentric in focusing on marginal or incomplete membership in the white world—assuming the precedence of the white world over the black. Thus, the very use of such a word obscures the possible richness that exists in "the other world." This conception, which is primarily concerned with membership in the white world (mainstream) and drawing attention to what blacks do not have in the white world, posits that the values of belonging to this world outweigh those of belonging to any other. In fact, it does not even consider that there is noteworthy value in having an other-culture membership. Although it is true that the bulk of wealth and power in this society is in the hands of those who have solid membership in the mainstream (white males), and therefore the potential value of membership in the mainstream cannot be denied, the lack of recognition of any possible value in membership in a minority community involves a problem of perspective. This conception has often assumed that lack of full membership in mainstream society is equivalent to and intrinsically linked to mental illness including schizophrenia (Kardiner & Ovesey, 1949). In a very real sense, this problem extends beyond the context of Anglocentrism, male-centrism, and capitalism, to racism. This subcultural membership, in fact, embodies enviable sources of strength (black family, membership in the black community) for the so-called "marginal" black American.

The traditional view of the concept of marginality is a limited one as is shown in the case of blacks in corporate America. A revised, broader view, one that takes into account not just the possible negative aspects, needs to be considered. Blacks in the middle class who occupy elite status positions for their race are very much tied to the black community. They are not divorced from but rather are participants in the black subculture, and there are benefits that they derive from their subcultural membership. Managers and their spouses have attested to their continued ties to extended family and extended family networks of support, their involvement in black civic and social organizations, and strong ties of friendship and regular relationships with other blacks.

At the same time, black corporate managers are active participants in mainstream culture. They speak the language of the business world, were educated in mainstream institutions of higher education including Ivy League colleges and universities, and enjoy various material aspects of mainstream culture. "Cultural bilingualism" thus enables black corporate families to enjoy the benefits of membership in both worlds—especially supportive kinship and social networks from within the subculture, and economic strength and acumen from the mainstream.

The concept of multiculturalism—the ability to understand and appreciate other cultures, their experiences and perspectives on the world—over the past more than a decade has been a topic of debate in the spheres of education and work (Fernandez, 1993; Griggs, Copeland Productions, 1987; Kenton, 1997; Ponterotto & Pedersen, 1993; Rogers, 1996; Tayeb, 1996). In progressive-minded circles of discussion on this subject, a positive value is placed on working toward achieving a truly multicultural workplace, educational environment, society, and so on. It would appear that black corporate and other black middle-class families would be at the forefront in achieving a multicultural identity.

In recent decades, family studies scholars have identified several perspectives, including some nonpejorative perspectives, from which difference can be viewed (see Adams, 1995; Allen, 1978, 1986; Mathis, 1978; H. P. McAdoo, 1988, 1993; Nobles, 1978; Peters, 1981, 1988; Staples & Mirande, 1980; Taylor, Chatters, Tucker, & Lewis, 1990; Wilkinson, 1978; Willie, 1988, 1991b). The pervasiveness and the power of the historical tendency in our society to consider that which is different as deviant, however, is evidenced by U.S. social, economic, and political treatment of ethnic and racial minorities, women, and those with alternative sexual orientations. This "difference = deviance" perspective has often blinded us to recognizing the positive aspects of other social groups. In short, in the case of black corporate managers and their families, there are positive as well as negative aspects of being different.

10

Summary, Conclusions, and Discussion

In this chapter, I will attempt to bring to closure the questions that guided and the issues that were raised in this research. A critique of the research and its limitations will be offered with suggestions for further research. The chapter will close with discussion of some issues raised and some explicit and implicit implications of the project. Let us begin by taking a look at the original aims and questions that directed the course of this work.

What Was Attempted, What Was Found

In this work, I have attempted to broadly examine the sources of stress for and the strengths of black families in corporate America. I also delved into the ways in which race is a causal factor in shaping the lives of black corporate managerial families. I tried to look at the family as a unit as well as its individual members and dyadic components.

The families' link to the corporation via employment in management of (at least) one of the family heads, and all that this holds in general and on a day-to-day basis uniquely affected the families as a whole. It also affected, by adding stress and by enlisting families' strengths, each of its individual members. The sources and nature of stress were different for these families as were the particular set of strengths that bolstered them. A big part of this difference is attributable to race.

The stresses of racism and tokenism appear to be pervasive in the lives of black corporate managers and their families. Respondents stated that racism remains a highly persistent variable in their lives. These "isms" negatively impact managers' marginal status, upward mobility, and social relations on the job. They also create problems for managers and their families in relation to areas such as mate selection and other interpersonal relationships, child rearing, and the experience of relocation. In short, they affect the lives of managers, their spouses, their children, and these families, in general. It therefore becomes essential when constructing a family stress model to build in the components of racism and tokenism as core elements of the model.

But black corporate families also have a set of cultural strengths that bolster them. The hypothesis asserting the prevalence of the black family strengths of a strong work orientation, adaptability of family roles, a strong achievement orientation, a strong religious orientation, and strong kinship bonds identified by Robert Hill (1971) was supported. Families attested to the presence of all five black family cultural strengths in their experiences. These strengths as well as membership in a black social cultural community (also proposed as a strength) were present and operative in these families. There were no families in this study who could be classified as weak in a general sense. These families were special, strong, and fortunate—special for all that they have achieved, strong in the abundance of strengths that they have, and fortunate for possessing the intelligence, skill, luck, and family support to be successful in corporate America.

MIDDLE-CLASS BLACK FAMILY ISSUES

Black corporate managerial families are a select case among black middle-class families. Because they form a sizable part of that group (black middle-class families), they share much the same life experiences, worries, and sources of stress. In this book, we have touched on several of these.

Black middle-class parents have special concerns for their children. Because their income affords them a better quality of life regarding type of home, neighborhood, and schools, this often means that their children grow up without regular contact with significant numbers of other black children. How to prevent "whitewashing" or the eradication of the

"African Americaness" of their children's sense of self becomes a concern. Black adults too, in most cases, lament their own estrangement from other blacks, who are largely absent in their communities. The question that is raised for black corporate managerial and other black middle-class families becomes "Middle-class lifestyle at what cost?"

Middle-class blacks, like others, continue to suffer from racism in the workplace. Despite the gains and struggles of the past few decades, we continue to hear stories of unequal treatment and denied opportunities that are attributed to race. Those blacks who do enjoy a modicum of career success are almost sure to suffer isolation from other blacks as they continue their move to the top of their career ladders, and they are also likely to have their authority and ability second guessed.

Successful black women have an additional set of problems. If they are single, their success seems to estrange them from single black men, whom they have in many instances outdistanced professionally, and thus their chances for involvement in male-female interpersonal relationships become limited. Furthermore, they still must cope with sexism and racism in their own upward climb. For those women who are wives and mothers as well as workers, the problems of sexism and racism are merely added to the already burdensome task of juggling work and domestic roles, which are further complicated by their appreciation of the experiences of racism encountered by their husbands and children, and the need to derive strategies to help deal with these problems.

THE DIFFERENCE OF RACE

If "it is all a matter of perspective" as Willie (1978) contends, then race persists as a salient factor in the lives of black corporate managers and their families. From the vantage point of these men and women as well as from that of the objective observer, life experiences of these middle-class black individuals both on and off the job are qualitatively different than those of their white counterparts as based on race. Some of these differences are positive. Here I am referring to the particular sources of strength—familial, community, and otherwise, that black corporate families have from which to draw. Some of the differences stem from the negatives of racism and the myriad of ways in which this "ism" persists in adversely affecting their lives. In U.S. society today, race still functions as a social and economic stratifier, and differential treatment and opportunities are afforded to members of this society on the basis of race. Some of the differences are simply that.

The men and women who are the subjects of this book are among the successes within black America. They are the achievers in educational achievement, occupational status, and income. They are part of what W. E. B. Du Bois (1967) would have referred to as today's "talented tenth" among black Americans. Yet, although they have overcome the barriers of legal segregation that prohibited the upward social mobility of their parents and grandparents, racism, which remains at the core of the social and institutional arrangements of our society, continues to stymie their climb toward greater social, economic, and psychological well-being—theirs and that of their children. Race is not declining but remains a highly potent factor in determining the life chances and experiences of black Americans and white Americans even, and perhaps especially, in the middle class.

Limitations, Improvements, Suggestions for Future Research

Although it is my hope that this research is powerfully insightful and identifies many of the sources of stress and strengths of black corporate families as a special group of middle-class black families, there is always room for improvement. Furthermore, the research process suggested several new, important, and interesting issues and questions to explore. The following are suggestions for improvement and directions for further research.

ASSESSMENT OF THE STRENGTH OF FAMILIES AND IDENTIFICATION OF FAMILY STRENGTHS

As was previously mentioned, there were no truly weak families found among those in the sample. Use of an instrument that could yield a better assessment of strength—for example, one that could discriminate among or delineate degrees of strength—would offer an improvement. Identification of additional strengths to those included in this research would also be valuable. Although Robert Hill's (1971) list of strengths is still useful, it is not totally adequate. As was suggested in

Chapter 2, a more dynamic approach to the study, with a definition and a clearer understanding of family strengths, is sorely needed. The use of FACES II (Olson & McCubbin, 1983, 1989) is suggested to assist with these concerns (although perhaps with some modifications and additions). FACES II has been used with some success with black families; however, it has not been widely tested with that population. In addition, it would be useful to know when and how these strengths developed, for example, through the family of origin via early childhood socialization processes (as is likely to be the case with Hill's traditional black family strengths), through necessity, or other experiences. Furthermore, quantification and better operationalization of family strengths could move the data in the direction of greater objectivity.

IMPROVED SAMPLING TECHNIQUE

Although still wedded to the value of qualitative analysis, the use of a more methodologically rigorous sampling technique might be considered. Such would function to improve validity and ensure greater generalizability of findings to the broader population under study. Use of a stratified random sample would offer these improvements.

THE NATURE OF INFORMAL NETWORKS OF SUPPORT

A deeper exploration into how and why belonging to a black "community" supports and assists families, especially in the relocation experience, would be useful. Although respondents attested that relocation has its host of difficulties, the informal support networks—familial, social, and otherwise—eased the experience. There is a need for greater specification of these and the answers to such questions as, What is their power? How strong are they? Is one type (e.g., civil, social, fraternal, church related) stronger than another? These are important issues to answer and address.

RACIAL AWARENESS PARENTING STRATEGIES

This research strongly suggests the need for the development of more concrete research-based parenting strategies regarding racial awareness. We need to further develop the new and emerging literature on how to raise a multicultural child. But more specific to this research, we need to develop the research-based literature on how to raise a racially aware middle-class African American child.

THE REASONS FOR AND TIMING OF DIVORCE

The research instrument was not sensitive enough to discern whether those in the sample who occupy the status of divorced achieved that status before entering versus during corporate managerial employ. If it is the case that divorce occurs while employed in corporate management or while moving up the ranks to managerial status, some questions for further research might include the following: Does the higher divorce rate status among female black corporate managers result from the feeling of a threat posed to their husbands' sense of self-worth by their wives' high levels of success? Do the demands of corporate managerial employment yield higher divorce rates especially for female black managers but for black managers in general? Knowing the causes of divorce for this group might open up possibilities for solutions.

REQUISITE EGO STRENGTH

It would seem that high levels of ego strength among black corporate managers, and especially male black managers, as they enjoy higher levels of success compared with black females in the corporate world, are absolutely necessary for survival in corporate America. Extraordinary ego strength is needed to bolster them against the persistent and pervasive forms of racism that they are subjected to on the climb up the corporate ladder as well as in the broader social environment, including experiences beginning in early childhood. Research would do well to examine the cultural ways in which black women, the primary caregivers of young black children, arm them (boys especially) with an almost unflappable sense of self-confidence in the face of the frequent bombardment of racial assault that has been proven to be generally ego damaging.

FAMILY STRENGTHS RESEARCH IN THE FUTURE

I would like to suggest the development of a stress-combative model of family strengths as a future direction for family strengths research. In this attempt, I posit that there are three important ways of looking at family strengths to keep in mind.

1. There are some things or events that all families are likely to experience.
2. There are differences in family experience by race, class, family structure, and other categorical or group distinctions.
3. Any given family will have its own unique combination of individual experiences.

For research on family strengths to be comprehensive, the subject of family strengths then must be viewed by looking at stress on these three levels. There is value in researching all three. Although we need research that addresses strengths on each of these levels, it is the last two levels that I highlight as most important for further research.

Let me include one final caution worth reiterating that was previously addressed elsewhere in the literature about how we should view family strengths from a stress-combative perspective. Important to any discussion or definition of strengths is the individual's self-definitions of an experience or crisis as being stressful or not, and to what extent. Prescriptions for wellness and strengths, to be adequate, must take into account the meanings that the potential stressor holds for the particular family involved.

Although there are many questions left unanswered about the determination of family strengths, various researchers have explored the area. But their search for answers about family strengths needs to focus more on the interaction between the circumstances and stresses any given family faces and the resources that that family has to cope with them. Prescriptions for strengthening families must be devised in light of the difficulties that all families are likely to encounter, but also by accounting for differences in family experiences by culture, race, and other factors and, also important, with an eye toward the unique multiplicity of variation that individual families will face.

Discussion: Building the New Corporate Enterprise—Diversity and Responsibility

During the remainder of this decade and beyond, we will continue to witness the "browning" of America as blacks, Hispanics, and Asians increase their numbers and proportions in the general population. In the next 40 to 50 years, it is estimated that national demographics will change so that people of color will make up close to 50% of the total population. Furthermore, women and minorities will comprise the majority of new entrants to the workforce.

The questions that this phenomenon raises for corporate America are rich and complex. Diversity in the population and the workforce has powerful fiscal implications that suggest that racism in our society must be seriously revisited. It will add to the complicated nature of family today. It will give new meaning to and increase the scope of corporate responsibility. A sensitive and quality approach to each of these areas of impact will be extremely important for securing a successful future for corporate America, particularly at a time when we are rapidly losing our competitive edge in the global marketplace.

Blacks and minorities are still today a vastly underused resource. The fact that their talents and abilities, unique and otherwise, have not been extensively tapped is no less a folly than would be wasting any other resource. Their inclusion would equal a "value added" and this fact needs to be recognized.

VALUING DIVERSITY IS IMPORTANT

In a very real sense, we can say that recently blacks in middle management have been losing ground. The gains of equal employment opportunity and affirmative action are being lost in the corporate workforce; companies have and continue to downsize, and although some whites have been let go, blacks have been fired at a disproportionately higher rate.

Job areas nonessential to profit or the key function of the organization, for example, personnel, have been hard hit. These are also the areas that blacks (and women) have been routinely funneled into.

We must also consider the negative impact on blacks just coming into and up the corporate ranks. For them, this means a loss of role models and mentors. Many corporations seem to be missing sight of this valuable human resource, which has proven thus far to significantly contribute to profit and productivity. Some of the best performers, with respect to sales and revenues, in many of the nation's top corporations are blacks and other minorities.

What Needs to Be Done

Companies need not only boast of meeting affirmative action quotas or of having a good track record regarding hiring. They must also educate those within their ranks, especially whites and males, about participation in a diverse work environment if such a workforce is to be managed effectively. Although blacks may be a permanent presence in corporate America and have had a place there, however tenuous, for more than two decades, prejudiced attitudes toward them and myths about them held by white workers still prevail. We need to revisit affirmative action and reinforce government monitoring of hiring practices. Without employee education in the form of diversity training and with the lessening of government commitment to affirmative action hiring practices, the number of blacks in high positions has begun to backslide. (Some companies that were good in the past in this regard have been less so recently.)

THE PROBLEM OF CULTURAL BAGGAGE

All of us who are born and reared in the United States are socialized into American culture. What we often fail to recognize, however, is that this socialization process, which begins in our homes and our neighborhoods, typically exposes us to only a very narrow slice or subculture of American society and its norms and values (Elkin & Handel, 1989). Because of the relatively limited context in which this process occurs, according to Elkin and Handel, "every child's socialization in some measure limits his or her ability to function in a larger society" (1987, p. 81). What we value, approve of, and view as the norm is shaped by an insular set of experiences. We develop an ethnocentric and egocentric view of the world. Our ability to value more broadly persons and experiences that are different from our own is significantly hampered.

Scholars used to be very one-sided in their thinking here. They used to say that blacks from their particular subcultural background or backgrounds could not function easily or well in white middle-class society. Now they also recognize and admit that white middle-class individuals are often constrained and locked in by their values and norms and do not recognize that there are other perspectives and ways of doing things.

Education in corporate America needs to take place to heighten awareness and sensitivity to other groups. White managers need to talk about race and race-related issues. Limited socialization experiences in childhood and adulthood including those in the workplace render many white managers socially incompetent in a world that is increasingly more diverse.

BUILDING PARTNERSHIPS

Mentoring is an important strategy for increasing the numbers of blacks and other minorities at higher levels of corporate management. What all newcomers to the corporation need is access to information and support. Top managers need to take an interest in the individual career development of new young black hirees. This is a tried-and-true method for ensuring their success. Partnerships at the highest levels down through the ranks serve to build a strong organization. Time spent by senior managers in grooming those their junior must be viewed as an investment in the company's human resources. Therefore, corporations should institute initiatives to encourage such relations. According to David Kerns, former CEO, Xerox Corporation, "The company that successfully manages diversity will have the competitive edge."

THE COMPLICATED NATURE OF FAMILY TODAY

The family, still one of the most fundamental social institutions, becomes an increasingly more difficult one to define. Over the past more than three decades, the family in transition has challenged our notions of the content of family roles, power dimensions, the allocation of time and other scarce resources, and structure. At the same time, its sources of stress and support also have changed.

As this period of transition began, the literature informs us that with the addition of new dimensions to the at one time more unitary nature of families, many hoped the changes would be temporary. Some feared they would be permanent. Others eagerly embraced the spirit of change, recognizing the family as ripe for such an occurrence.

The simple fact is that family is more complicated today. High technology has had a multiplicity of impacts on how families function. Media, especially television, now shape our notions of family, determine how we spend our leisure time, and educate (for better and for worse) as well as baby-sit our children. "Child care by chance" characterizes how we as a nation care for our children. The problems affecting youngsters now include monumental ills such as crack/cocaine use, alcohol abuse, and AIDS.

Simultaneously, marriages and families are increasingly dual-worker headed, the nuclear family structure comprises fewer than a third of all U.S. families, more than half of mothers with children under one year of age are employed, and single-parent families proliferate (Bernard, 1975a; Skolnick & Skolnick, 1992). These are the new facts about our families in the 1990s.

Although poverty affects a startling proportion of our families today, with some asserting that more Americans are plagued with this condition than have been seen since the Great Depression, more U.S. families than ever before have achieved middle-class status. For these middle-class families, economic factors and all of these other factors of change will create new opportunities and new stressors. For these, the majority of U.S. families, the focus of concerns, in a very real sense, shifts an increasing emphasis to factors related to psychosocial well-being versus basic survival issues.

The components of our society on the most micro as well as macro levels will be required to rise to the challenge of supporting family in its new reality. Business is no exception. As the nature of family changes, so must the nature of corporate responsibility.

CORPORATE RESPONSIBILITY: THE NEED FOR A NEW DEFINITION

Although corporate responsibility has taken on many faces, large corporations have traditionally added to their business vision agendas of social responsibility, and charitable commitment, philanthropic commitment, or both. Many corporations have focused efforts and resources in this connection on a single area of concern such as public education, or Third World development. Others direct efforts more broadly. In either case, what often comes to mind when the term *corporate responsibility* is used is corporate efforts that extend concerns external to the corporation. Thus, corporate responsibility is frequently defined as addressing persons, problems, or projects that do not directly affect company personnel.

External social responsibility efforts are important; however, corporate responsibility should extend to include more often those closest to home: the corporation's employees. Although the major U.S. corporations have somewhat extensive employee assistance programs to attend to employee needs, and corporations offer benefits of a variety of types (vacation, sick leave, and so on), practices of these programs and the operative notions behind them are not conceptually synonymous with corporate responsibility. If we redefine corporate responsibility to include corporate workers, motivation for benefit practices and programs changes. In turn, the realization of corporate responsibility extended to include employees is not only happier, healthier employees, but also more productive workers, which translates into profits for the corporation.

SPECIAL ISSUES AND PROBLEMS WITH RELOCATION

Contemporary corporate managers raise three new issues for companies to consider in the business of corporate relocation, the topic explored in Chapter 6. They are, first, that women work, and sometimes do so as corporate managers. They bring with them to the workplace their own styles and priorities. Second, the population of corporate managers has increased in its diversity with respect to race and ethnicity, with varied personal preferences and needs that stem from membership in the various subcultures of the United States. And, third, managers are less willing to let the company interfere with family life. The prototypical "company man" has become extinct; so, too, has the willingness among many managers to put the company first to the detriment of one's family's well-being. These are the new issues and problems facing corporations today regarding relocation.

Furthermore, families today have become more egalitarian. This reality is out of sync with the fact that spouses, especially if they are wives, and children most often bear the brunt of the problems associated with relocation. Increased consideration and respect for the integrity of all family members must be given.

We might also point out that the American family since the turn of the century has become more specialized in its functions. In particular, over the past two decades, middle-class American families, having achieved a level of comfort and security regarding the basic bread-and-butter issues of quality food, clothing, and shelter, can now focus more of their attention on meeting the interpersonal, psychosocial needs of its members. This decrease in the dichotomization of the instrumental and expressive family functions renders a more integrated pattern of functioning, and a more cohesive and singular perspective on personal and family maintenance and well-being.

Some companies have begun to recognize the changing needs of contemporary corporate families. Several of the major corporations have relocation programs to assist the manager and his or her family in the relocation process. Such programs vary in the help they provide, and range from assistance in facilitating the move to assisting spouses in finding new employment, to seminars to orient managers and their families to the new community. Some programs are better than others, but all need to increase their sensitivity to the problems of relocation for not just the employee but also for the families involved. Companies must further extend the notion of corporate responsibility to the workers who serve them and to their families, and begin to show an awareness of and to address the unique problems and needs of different types of workers including singles, blacks and other racial minorities, and women, and their respective families.

The nature of work, family, and life in general in the 1990s results in a shared set of problems and concerns for the labor force. Concerns with regard to job and economic stability, relocation of workers and their families, and child care among families with children are some of these shared concerns. But although there are commonalities of concern among all families, there are also different ones for those workers who differ from the mainstream of workers on the basis of sex, race, and ethnicity. If we use blacks and their experiences with relocation as an example—the problems of uprooting children from cultural connections essential for their healthy development as black youngsters, moving single black females in particular to geographic regions that are characterized by a dearth of black men thus limiting the mate selection possibilities, and distancing black individuals and families from community, civic, social, and religious organizations and institutions including the black church—in light of the special significance of these in black life and, indeed, black psychosocial survival, the case for differences of concern is made. Corporations could help a great deal by being sensitive to the array of issues that exist for all of their employees and being flexible and assisting with these transitions and concerns.

Conclusion

This book attempts to identify some of the sources of stress and strengths of black corporate managers and their families. It has tried to point out some of the factors that were causal of the success of blacks in this group, as well as some of the factors that were obstacles to still greater achievement. In addition, I have tried to provide a glimpse of the day-to-day concerns of these managers, their spouses, and their children, and what enables them to hold it all together. More important, this book suggests areas for further investigation by scholars and practitioners interested in developing the theoretical and practical tools for building and supporting the strengths and overall well-being of these and similar middle-class black families. For corporate America, this book should provide further incentive to appreciate the struggles as well as the talents of a highly under-utilized human resource.

It is hoped that these aims have and will be achieved.

Appendix A

Content and Organization of Manager's Interview Questionnaire

1. Personal Data
2. Background Information (antecedent factors)
3. Corporate Demands
4. Work Environment
5. Community
6. Family Strengths
   a. Support From Kin/Kinship Bonds
   b. Adaptability of Family Roles
   c. Religious Orientation
   d. Achievement Orientation
   e. Role Flexibility
7. Family Stress
8. Wives' Incorporation

Appendix B

Items Assessing Five Traditional Black Family Strengths

Work Orientation

- On an average, how many evenings per week do you work late?
- How often do you travel out of town on company business?

Adaptability of Family Roles

- How many evenings during the week do you spend time with your children?
- How often are you the sole supervisor of your children's activities?
- Describe how this time is spent.
- Which of the following activities do you engage in with your children on a regular basis?
  a. Giving child a bath
  b. Reading a story
  c. Checking homework
  d. Putting child to bed
  e. Transporting to lessons, scout meeting, other activities
- Do you share in the household chores?
- Are there household chores that you perform on a regular basis?
- If so, which ones?
- Did your mother ever work when you were a child?
- Does she work now?
- Did other women in your family work? (excluding spouse)

172

- Did your spouse's mother work when your wife was a child?
- Does she work now?
- Did other women in your spouse's family work?

Achievement Orientation

- Do you aspire to further promotions or upward career moves within or outside of your company?
- How would you compare your level of success to that with those with whom you grew up?
- To what do you attribute your success? (indicate as many things as are applicable)

Religious Orientation

- As a child, did you and any members of your family attend church?
- Same for spouse?
- If so, how often?
- Do you attend church now?
- If so, how often?
- Do your children attend church?
- Do you consider yourself to be a religious person?

Kinship Bonds

- Among your relatives, excluding your spouse, is there someone you can turn to for advice, understanding, or support?
- How often do you communicate with family members living outside your household?
- How often do you see relatives who live outside of your household?
- How far away do you reside from members of your family?
- Are there at present, or have there been in the past, relatives other than your spouse and children (including those by a previous relationship) residing in your household?
  a. If yes, who?
  b. For how long?
  c. Was (is) this a permanent arrangement?
- Do you receive any kind of help or support from family members?
- In what ways do family members help you? List as many as applicable. (financial, emotional, child care, advice, and so on)

- Describe the frequency of help or support, on any level, that you receive.
- How important is their help to you, or how important do you consider their help and support to be in your life?
- Is support within your kinship network reciprocal? Explain.
- Did your family assist you financially with your education?
- From which of the following sources do you receive the most support?
  a. Family
  b. Friends
  c. Community or service agencies

References

Adams, B. N. (1995). *The family: A sociological interpretation.* Fort Worth, TX: Harcourt Brace.

Allen, W. R. (1978). The search for applicable theories of black family life. *Journal of Marriage and the Family, 40*(1), 117-129.

Allen, W. R. (1986). *Black American families 1965-1984: A classified selectively annotated bibliography.* Westport, CT: Greenwood.

Ambert, A.-M., Adler, P. A., Adler, P., & Detzner, D. F. (1995). Understanding and evaluating qualitative research. *Journal of Marriage and the Family, 57,* 879-893.

America, R. F. (1978). *Moving ahead: Black managers in American business.* New York: McGraw-Hill.

Ammons, P., Nelson, J., & Wodarski, J. (1982). Surviving corporate moves: Sources of stress and adaptation among corporate executive families. *Family Relations, 31,* 207-212.

Apter, T. E. (1994). *Working women don't have wives.* New York: St. Martin's.

Archer, J. (1969). *Achieve executive success, avoid family failure.* New York: Grosset & Dunlap.

Bailey, D., Wolfe, D., & Wolfe, C. R. (1996). The contextual impact of social support across race and gender. *Journal of Black Studies, 26,* 287-307.

Banks, J. A. (1984). Black youths in predominantly white suburbs: An exploratory study of their attitudes and self-concepts. *Journal of Negro Education, 53,* 1.

Barnes, A. S. (1985). *The black middle-class family: A study of black subsociety, neighborhood, and home in interaction.* Bristol, IN: Wyndham Hall.

Bartz, K. W., & LeVine, E. S. (1978). Child rearing by black parents: A description and comparison to Anglo and Chicano parents. *Journal of Marriage and the Family, 40,* 709.

Baumrind, D. (1972). An exploratory study of socialization effects on black children: Some black-white comparisons. *Child Development, 43,* 261-267.

Benedict, R. (1934). *Patterns of culture.* Boston: Houghton Mifflin.

Bernard, J. (1975a). *Women, wives, mothers.* Chicago: Aldine.

Bernard, J. (1975b). Adolescence and socialization for motherhood. In S. E. Dragastin & G. H. Elder (Eds.), *Adolescence in the life cycle* (pp. 227-252). New York: John Wiley.

Bernstein, P. (1985). *Family ties, corporate bond.* Garden City, NY: Doubleday.

Berretta, R. (1982). *The pursuit of family strength.* Fresno, CA: Statewide.

Billingsley, A. (1968). *Black families in white America.* Englewood Cliffs, NJ: Prentice Hall.

Blassingame, J. W. (1972). *The slave community.* New York: Oxford University Press.

Blau, F., & Ehrenberg, R. C. (Eds.). (1997). *Gender and family issues in the workplace.* New York: Russell Sage.

Blauner, R. (1972). *Racial oppression in America.* New York: Harper & Row.

Blumer, H. (1969). *Symbolic interactionism.* Englewood Cliffs, NJ: Prentice Hall.

Blumer, H. (1982). Industrialization and race relations. In N. R. Yetman & C. H. Steele (Eds.), *Majority and minority* (pp. 54-65). Boston: Allyn & Bacon.

Brewer, J., & Hunter, A. (1989). *Multimethod research: A synthesis of styles.* Newbury Park, CA: Sage.

Boss, P., McCubbin, H., & Lester, G. (1979). The corporate executive wife's coping patterns in response to routine husband-father absence. *Family Process, 18*(1), 79-86.

Boyd, R. L. (1991). Black entrepreneurship in 52 metropolitan areas. *Sociology and Social Research, 75,* 158-163.

Broman, C. L. (1991). Gender, work-family roles, and psychological well-being of blacks. *Journal of Marriage and the Family, 53,* 509-520.

Bureau of Labor Statistics. (1980). *Statistical abstract of the United States.* Washington, DC: U.S. Department of Commerce.

Bureau of Labor Statistics. (1990). *Statistical abstract of the United States.* Washington, DC: U.S. Department of Commerce.

Bureau of Labor Statistics. (1995). *Statistical abstract of the United States.* Washington, DC: U.S. Department of Commerce.

Carson, C., Garrow, D. J., Harding, V., Hine, D. C. (Eds.). (1987). *Eyes on the prize* [Audio program]. New York: Viking/Penguin.

Centers, R. (1975). Attitude similarity-dissimilarity as a correlate of heterosexual attraction and love. *Journal of Marriage and the Family, 37,* 305-312.

Chodorow, N. (1978). *The reproduction of mothering: Psychoanalysis and the sociology of gender.* Berkeley: University of California Press.

Clark, R. (1983). *Family life and school achievement: Why poor black children succeed or fail.* Chicago: University of Chicago Press.

Collins, R., & Makowsky, M. (1993). *The discovery of society* (5th ed.). New York: McGraw-Hill.

Collins, S. (1979). Making ourselves visible: Evolution of career status and self-image of minority professional women. In L. A. Geiselman (Ed.), *The minority woman in America: Professionalism at what cost?* (pp. 4-14). San Francisco: University of California Press.

Comer, J. P., & Poussaint, A. F. (1975). *Raising black children.* New York: Penguin.

Comer, J. P., & Poussaint, A. F. (1992). *Raising black children* (2nd ed.). New York: Penguin.

Connell, J. P., Spencer, M. B., & Aber, J. L. (1994). Educational risk and resilience in African American youth: Content, self, action, and outcomes in school. *Child Development, 65,* 493-506.

Crouter, A. C. (1984). Spillover from family to work: The neglected side of the work-family interface. *Human Relations, 37,* 425-442.

Curran, D. (1983). *Traits of a healthy family.* Minneapolis, MN: Winston.

Davis, B. L. (1995). African American family resources for coping: The dance of stress. In R. W. Johnson (Ed.), *African American voices: African American health educators speak out.* New York: National League for Nursing Press.

Davis, G., & Watson, G. (1982). *Black life in corporate America.* Garden City, NY: Anchor Press/Doubleday.

Davis, L. G. (1986). *The black family in the United States: A revised, updated selectively annotated bibliography.* Westport, CT: Greenwood.

Demause, L. (1974). *The history of childhood.* New York: Random.

Demos, V. (1990). Black family studies in the *Journal of Marriage and the Family* and the issue of distortion: A trend analysis. *Journal of Marriage and the Family, 52,* 603-612.

Dickins, F., & Dickins, J. (1982). *The black manager: Making it in the corporate world.* New York: AMACOM.

Dinnerstein, M. (1992). *Women between two worlds: Midlife reflection on work and family.* Philadelphia, PA: Temple University Press.

Dohrenwend, B., & Dohrenwend, B. (Eds.). (1974). *Stressful life events: Their nature and effects.* New York: John Wiley.

Dorothy Height on racism and interpersonal relationships. (1986, May 29). *USA Today,* p. 5D.

Dransfield, A. (1984, August 20). The uneasy life of the corporate spouse. *Fortune, 110,* 26-32.

Du Bois, W. E. B. (1908). *The Negro American family.* Atlanta, GA: Atlanta University Press.

Du Bois, W. E. B. (1967). *The Philadelphia Negro: A social study.* New York: Schocken. (Original work published in 1899)

Durkheim, E. (1964). *The division of labor in society.* New York: Free Press. (Original work published in 1893)

Eckenrode, J., & Gore, S. (Eds.). (1990). *Stress between work and family.* New York: Plenum Press.

Elkin, F., & Handel, G. (1987). *The child and society* (4th ed.). New York: Random.

Elkin, F., & Handel, G. (1989). *The child and society* (5th ed.). New York: Random.

Ellison, C. G. (1990). Family ties, friendships, and subjective well-being among black Americans. *Journal of Marriage and the Family, 52,* 298-310.

Elman, M. R., & Gilbert, L. A. (1984). Coping strategies for role conflict in married professional women with children. *Family Relations, 33,* 317-327.

Epstein, C. (1971). Law partners and marital partners: Strains and solutions in the dual career family enterprise. *Human Relations, 24,* 544-563.

Epstein, C. (1973). Positive effects of the multiple negative: Explaining the success of black professional women. *American Journal of Sociology, 78,* 913-935.

Feagin, J. R., & Sikes, M. P. (1994). *Living with racism: The black middle-class experience.* Boston: Beacon.

Fein, R. (1978). Research on fathering: Social policy and an emergent perspective. *Journal of Social Issues, 34*(1), 122-135.

Feldman, S. S., & Elliott, G. R. (1990). *At the threshold: The developing adolescent.* Cambridge, MA: Harvard University Press.

Fernandez, J. P. (1975). *Black managers in white corporations.* New York: John Wiley.

Fernandez, J. P. (1981). *Racism and sexism in corporate life.* Lexington, MA: D. C. Heath.

Fernandez, J. P. (1993). *The diversity advantage.* New York: Lexington.

Finch, J. (1983). *Married to the job: Wives' incorporation in men's work.* Winchester, MA: Allen and Unwin.

Fine, M., Schewebel, A. I., & James-Myers, L. (1987). Family stability in black families: Values underlying three different perspectives. *Journal of Comparative Family Studies, 18*(1), 1-23.

Fishman, D. B., & Cherniss, C. (Eds.). (1990). *The human side of corporate competitiveness.* Newbury Park, CA: Sage.

Fox, M. F., & Hesse-Biber, S. (1984). *Women at work.* Palo Alto, CA: Mayfield.

Frazier, E. F. (1957). *Black bourgeoisie.* New York: Free Press.

Frazier, E. F. (1966). *The Negro family in the United States.* Chicago: University of Chicago Press. (Original work published in 1939)

Freeman, E. M. (1990). The black family's life cycle: Operationalizing a strengths perspective. In S. M. L. Logan, E. M. Freeman, & R. G. McRoy (Eds.), *Social work practice with black families* (pp. 35-72). New York: Longman.

Friedman, D. E. (1987). *Family-supportive policies: The corporate decision-making process.* New York: Conference Board.

Gambino, R. (1974). *Blood of my blood: The dilemma of the Italian Americans.* New York: Doubleday.

Gaylord, M. (1984). Relocation and the corporate family. In P. Voydanoff (Ed.), *Work and family* (pp. 144-152). Palo Alto, CA: Mayfield.

Genovese, E. (1972). *Roll Jordan roll.* New York: Random.

Gershenfeld, M. K. (1986). NETWORK: A program to strengthen black middle-class families. In P. W. Dail & R. H. Jewson (Eds.), *In praise of 50 years: The Groves conference on the conservation of marriage and the family* (pp. 54-62). Lake Mills, IA: Graphic Publishing.

Gerstel, N. R., & Gross, H. (1984). *Commuter marriage.* New York: Guilford.

Gherman, E. M. (1981). *Stress and the bottom line: A guide to personal well-being and corporate health.* New York: AMACOM.

Gilbert, L. A., Holahan, C. K., & Manning, L. (1981). Coping with conflict between professional and maternal roles. *Family Relations, 30,* 419-426.

Githens, M., & Prestage, J. (1977). *A portrait of marginality.* New York: David McKay.

Glick, P. C. 1997. Demographic pictures of African American families. In H. P. McAdoo (Ed.), *Black families* (3rd ed.), pp. 118-138. Thousand Oaks, CA: Sage.

Goffman, E. (1959). *The presentation of self in everyday life.* New York: Doubleday Anchor.

Goldscheider, F. K. (1991). The intergenerational flow of income: Family structure and the status of black Americans. *Journal of Marriage and the Family, 53,* 499-508.

Gordon, M. M. (1964). *Assimilation in American life: The role of race, religion, and national origins.* New York: Oxford University Press.

Greene, B. (1995). African American families. *Phi Kappa Phi Journal, 75*(3), 29-32.

Greiff, B. S., & Munter, P. (1980). *Tradeoffs: Executive, family, and organizational life.* New York: New American Library.

Griggs, Copeland Productions. (1987). *Valuing diversity.* San Francisco, CA: Author.

Gutman, H. G. (1976). *The black family in slavery and freedom 1750-1925.* New York: Random.

Hale-Benson, J. E. (1986). *Black children.* Baltimore, MD: Johns Hopkins University Press.

Hall, E. H., & King, G. C. (1982). Working with the strengths of black families. *Child Welfare, 61,* 536-544.

Hanks, R., & Sussman, M. B. (Eds). (1990). Corporations, businesses, and families [Special issue]. *Marriage and Family Review, 15.*

Hanson, S. M. H. (1986). Healthy single-parent families. *Family Relations, 35*(1), 125-132.

Harrison, A. O., & Minor, J. H. (1978). Interrole conflict, coping strategies, and satisfaction among black working wives. *Journal of Marriage and the Family, 40,* 799.

Hershberg, T., Burstein, A. N., Ericksen, E. P., Greenberg, S., & Yancey, W. L. (1979). A tale of three cities: Blacks, immigrants, and opportunity in Philadelphia: 1850-1880, 1930, and 1970. *Annals of the American Academy of Political and Social Science, 441,* 180-200.

Hill, R. (1949). *Families under stress.* New York: Harper.

Hill, R. (1965). Generic features of families under stress. In H. J. Parad (Ed.), *Crisis intervention: Selected readings* (pp. 32-52). New York: Family Service Association of America.

Hill, R. (1971). *The strengths of black families.* New York: Emerson Hall.

Holmes, T., & Rahe, R. (1967). The Social Readjustment Rating Scale. *Journal of Psychosomatic Research, 11,* 212-218.

Hopkins, E. (1987, January 19). Blacks at the top: Torn between two worlds. *New York Magazine,* 21-31.

Hopson, D. P., & Hopson, D. S. (1990). *Different and wonderful: Raising black children in a race-conscious society.* New York: Prentice Hall.

Hughes, E. (1949). Social change and status protest: An essay on the marginal man. *Phylon, 10,* 58-66.

Hunter College Women's Studies Collective. (1995). *Women's realities, women's choices* (2nd ed.). New York: Oxford University Press.

Hurd, E. P. (1995). Quiet success: Parenting strengths among African Americans. *Families in Society, 76,* 434-443.

In good company: Twenty-five best places for blacks to work. (1988). *Black Enterprise, 16,* 88-100.

Irons, E. D., & Moore, G. W. (1985). *Black managers: The case of the banking industry.* New York: Praeger.

Jayakody, R., Chatters, L. M., & Taylor, R. J. (1993). Family support to single and married African American mothers: The provision of financial, emotional, and child care assistances. *Journal of Marriage and the Family, 55,* 261-276.

Jaynes, G. D., & Williams, R. M. (Eds.). (1989). *A common destiny.* Washington, DC: National Academy Press.

Johnson, A. (1987). Black managers still have a dream. *Management Review, 76*(12), 20-24.

Jones, E. W., Jr. (1986). Black managers: The dream deferred. *Harvard Business Review, May/June*(3), 84-93.

Jones, R. L. (Ed.). (1989). *Black adolescents.* Berkley, CA: Cobb & Henry.

Kagan, J. (1976). The psychological requirements for human development. In N. B. Talbot (Ed.), *Raising children in modern America* (pp. 86-97). Boston: Little, Brown.

Kanter, R. M. (1977). *Men and women of the corporation.* New York: Basic Books.

Kardiner, A., & Ovesey, L. (1949). *The mark of oppression.* Cleveland, OH: World Publishing.

Kenton, S. B. (1997). *Crosstalk: Communicating in a multicultural workplace.* Upper Saddle River, NJ: Prentice Hall.

Kidder, L. H. (1981). *Research methods in social relations* (4th ed.). New York: Holt, Rinehart & Winston.

Kluwer, E., Heesink, José, & van de Vliert, E. (1996). Marital conflict about the division of household labor and paid work. *Journal of Marriage and the Family, 58,* 958-969.

Kofodimos, J. R. (1993). *Balancing act: How managers can integrate successful careers and fulfilling personal lives.* San Francisco, CA: Jossey-Bass.

Kozmetsky, R., & Kozmetsky, G. (1981). *Making it together: A survival manual for the executive family.* New York: Free Press.

Kutash, I., & Schlesinger, L. B. (Eds.). (1980). *Handbook on stress and anxiety.* San Francisco, CA: Jossey-Bass.

Ladner, J. (1971). *Tomorrow's tomorrow: The black woman.* Garden City, NY: Doubleday.

Landry, B. (1987). *The new black middle class.* Berkeley: University of California Press.

Lazarus, R. S. (1966). *Psychological stress and the coping process.* New York: McGraw-Hill.

Leggon, C. B. (1980). Black female professionals: Dilemmas and contradictions of status. In L. F. Rodgers-Rose (Ed.), *The black woman* (pp. 189-202). Beverly Hills, CA: Sage.

Lewis, J. M. (1979). *How's your family.* New York: Brunner Mazel.

Lincoln, C. E., & Mamiya, L. H. (1990). *The black church in the African American experience.* Durham, NC: Duke University Press.

Littlejohn-Blake, S. M., & Darling, C. A. (1993). Understanding the strengths of African American families. *Journal of Black Studies, 23,* 460-471.

Malmaud, K. (1984). *Work and marriage: Two-profession couple.* Ann Arbor, MI: UMI Research Press.

Mann, J. (1982, August 2). What is TV doing to America? *U.S. News and World Report,* p. 23.

Margolis, D. (1979). *The managers.* New York: William Morrow.

Mathis, A. (1978). Contrasting approaches to the study of black families. *Journal of Marriage and the Family, 40,* 667.

McAdoo, H., & McAdoo, J. L. (1985). *Black children: Social, educational, and parental environments.* Beverly Hills, CA: Sage.

McAdoo, H. P. (1978). Factors related to stability in upwardly mobile black families. *Journal of Marriage and the Family, 40,* 761-768.

McAdoo, H. P. (1979). Black kinship. *Psychology Today, 12,* 64.

McAdoo, H. P. (1981). *Black families.* Beverly Hills, CA: Sage.

McAdoo, H. P. (1988). *Black families* (2nd ed.). Newbury Park, CA: Sage.

McAdoo, H. P. (1993). *Family ethnicity: Strength in diversity.* Newbury Park, CA: Sage.

McAdoo, J. L. (1993). The roles of African American fathers: An ecological perspective. *Journal of Contemporary Human Services, 74,* 28-35.

McCoy, F. (1995). Shattering glass ceilings. *Black Enterprise, 23,* 22.

McCubbin, H., Boss, P., Wilson, L. R., & Lester, G. R. (1980). Developing family invulnerability to stress: Coping patterns and strategies wives employ in managing family separation. In J. Trost (Ed.), *The family in change* (pp. 79-86). Vasters, Sweden: International Library.

McCubbin, H., & McCubbin, M. (1988). Typologies of resilient families: Emerging roles of social class and ethnicity. *Family Relations, 37,* 247-254.

McCubbin, H., & Patterson, J. (1981). *Systematic assessment of family stress, resource, and coping: Tools for research, education, and clinical intervention.* St. Paul, MN: Family Social Science.

McCubbin, H., & Patterson, J. (1982). Family adaptation to crisis. In H. McCubbin, E. Cauble, & J. Patterson (Eds.), *Family stress, coping, and social support.* Springfield: Charles C Thomas.

McCubbin, H., & Patterson, J. (1983). The family stress process: A double ABCX model of adjustment and adaptation. In H. McCubbin, M. Sussman, & J. Patterson (Eds.), *Advances and developments in family stress theory and research* (pp. 7-37). New York: Haworth.

McLoyd, V. C. (1990). Minority children. *Child Development, 61,* 263-266.

Menaghan, E. G., & Parcel, T. L. (1990). Parental employment and family life: Research in the 1980s. *Journal of Marriage and the Family, 52,* 1079-1098.

Michaels, B. (1992). *Solving the work-family puzzle.* Homewood, IL: Business One Irwin.

Moen, P. (1983). The two-provider family: Problems and potentials. *Family Studies Review Yearbook, 1,* 397-427.

Morgan, T. (1985, October 27). The world ahead: Black parents prepare their children for pride and prejuidice. *New York Times Magazine,* 32.

Moynihan, D. P. (1965). *The Negro family: The case for national action.* Washington, DC: Government Printing Office.

Myrdal, G. (1944). *An American dilemma.* New York: Harper & Row.

Nixon, R. (1985a). *Climbing the corporate ladder: Some perceptions among black managers.* Washington, DC: National Urban League.

Nixon, R. (1985b). *Black managers in corporate America: Alienation or integration?* Washington, DC: National Urban League.

Nixon, R. (1985c). *Perceptions of job power among black managers in corporate America.* Washington, DC: National Urban League.

Nobles, W. W. (1974a). African root and American fruit: The black family. *Journal of Social and Behavioral Sciences, 20,* 66-77.

Nobles, W. W. (1974b). Africanity: Its role in black families. *Black Scholar, June,* 10-17.

Nobles, W. W. (1978). Toward an empirical and theoretical framework for defining black families. *Journal of Marriage and the Family, 40,* 679.

Olson, D., & McCubbin, H. (1983). *Families: What makes them work.* Beverly Hills, CA: Sage.

Olson, D., & McCubbin, H. (1989). *Families: What makes them work* (2nd ed.). Newbury Park, CA: Sage.

Otto, H. A. (1962). What is a strong family? *Marriage & Family Living, 24*(1), 77-81.

Otto, H. A. (1975). *The use of family strength concepts and methods in family life education.* Beverly Hills, CA: Holistic Press.

Papanek, H. (1973). Men, women, and work: Reflections on the two-person career. *American Journal of Sociology, 78,* 852-872.

Parad, H. J., & Caplan, G. (1965). A framework for studying families in crisis. In H. J. Parad (Ed.), *Crisis intervention: Selected readings* (pp. 53-72). New York: Family Service Association of America.

Park, R. E. (1928). Human migration and the marginal man. *American Journal of Sociology, 33,* 881-893.

Parsons, T., & Bales, R. F. (1955). *Family, socialization, and interaction process.* Glencoe, IL: Free Press.

Pearson, J. L. (1990). Black grandmothers in multigenerational households: Diversity in family structure and parenting involvement in the Woodlawn community. *Child Development, 61,* 434-442.

Peters, M. (1978). Notes from the guest editor. *Journal of Marriage and the Family, 40,* 655-658.

Peters, M. (1981). "Making it" black family style: Building on the strength of black families. In N. Stinnett, J. DeFrain, K. King, P. Knaub, & G. Rowe (Eds.), *Family strengths 3: Roots of well-being*. Lincoln: University of Nebraska Press.

Peters, M. (1988). Parenting in black families with young children: A historical perspective. In H. McAdoo (Ed.), *Black families* (2nd ed., pp. 211-224). Newbury Park, CA: Sage.

Piotrkowski, C. S., Rapoport, R. N., & Rapoport, R. (1987). Families and work. In M. B. Sussman & S. K. Steinmetz (Eds.), *Handbook of marriage and the family* (pp. 251-283). New York: Plenum.

Piotrkowski, C. S., & Repetti, R. L. (1984). Dual-earner families. *Marriage and Family Review, 7*(3/4), 99-124.

Pleck, J. H. (1977). The work-family role system. *Social Problems, 24*, 417-427.

Ponterotto, J. G., & Pedersen, P. B. (1993). *Preventing prejudice*. Newbury Park, CA: Sage.

Prus, R. (1996). *Symbolic interaction and ethnographic research*. Albany: State University of New York Press.

Redding, J. S. (1951). *On being Negro in America*. Indianapolis, IN: Bobbs-Merrill.

Richardson, L. (1981). *The dynamics of sex and gender* (2nd ed.). Boston: Houghton Mifflin.

Richardson, L. (1986). *The dynamics of sex and gender* (3rd ed.). Boston: Houghton Mifflin.

Riggs, B. A. (1990). Routine work-related absence: The effects on families. In M. Sussman (Ed.), *Marriage and family review* (pp. 147-160). New York: Haworth.

Robinson, B. H. (1995). *Where is my leading man?* Chicago: Hamilton Robinson Consultations.

Rodgers-Rose, L. (1980). *The black woman*. Beverly Hills, CA: Sage.

Rogers, M. F. (1996). *Multicultural experiences, multicultural theories*. New York: McGraw-Hill.

Ronnau, J. (1993). Identification and use of strengths: A family systems approach. *Children Today, 22*(2), 20-23.

Rosenblatt, P. C., Karis, T. A., & Powell, R. D. (1995). *Multiracial couples*. Thousand Oaks, CA: Sage.

Rossi, A. (1968). Transition to parenthood. *Journal of Marriage and the Family, 30*(1), 26-39.

Rossi, A. (1981). On the reproduction of mothering: A methodological debate. *Signs: Journal of Women in Culture and Society, 6*, 492-500.

Rubin, L. B. (1976). Blue-collar marriage and the sexual revolution. In L. B. Rubin (Ed.), *Worlds of pain: Life in the working-class family* (pp. 234-250). New York: Basic Books.

Sawin, M. M. (1979). *Family enrichment with family clusters*. Valley Forge, PA: Judson.

Schultz, N. C. (1991). Couple strengths and stressors in complex and simple stepfamilies in Australia. *Journal of Marriage and the Family, 53*, 555-564.

Seidenberg, R. (1973). *Corporate wives—Corporate casualties?* New York: Amacom.

Seifert, K., & Hoffnung, R. J. (1997). *Child and adolescent development* (4th ed.). Boston: Houghton Mifflin.

Selye, H. (1956). *The stress of life*. New York: McGraw-Hill.

Selye, H. (1974). *Stress without distress*. Philadelphia, PA: Lippincott.

Selye, H. (1983). *Selye's guide to stress research* (Vol. 2.) New York: Van Nostrand Reinhold.

Simmel, G. (1955). *Conflict and the web of group affiliations*. New York: Free Press.

Simpson, I. H., & England, P. (1981). Conjugal work roles and marital solidarity. *Journal of Family Issues, 2,* 180-204.

Skinner, D. A. (1983). Dual-career family stress and coping: A literature review. *Family Studies Review Yearbook, 1*(1), 127-133.

Skolnick, A., & Skolnick, J. (1986). *Family in transition* (5th ed.). Boston: Little, Brown.

Skolnick, A., & Skolnick, J. (1992). *Family in transition* (7th ed.). Boston: Little, Brown.

Smith, A., & Stewart, A. J. (1983). Approaches to studying racism and sexism in black women's lives. *Journal of Social Issues, 39*(3), 1-15.

Spanier, G. B. (1976). Measuring dyadic adjustment: New scales for assessing the quality of marriage and similar dyads. *Journal of Marriage and the Family, 38*(1), 15-28.

Spencer, M. B. (1976). The social-cognitive and study of personality development of the black preschool child: An exploratory development process. Unpublished doctoral dissertation, University of Chicago.

Spencer, M. B. (1988). Self-concept development. *New Directions, 3*(4), 59-72.

Spencer, M. B. (1990). Development of minority children: An introduction. *Child Development, 61,* 267-269.

Spencer, M. B., Brookins, G. K., & Allen, W. R. (1985). *Beginnings: The social and affective development of black children.* Hillsdale, NJ: Lawrence Erlbaum.

Spencer, M. B., Brookins, G. K., & Allen, W. R. (1991). Ethnicity, ethnic identity, and competence formation: Adolescent transition and cultural transformation. *Journal of Negro Education, 60,* 366-387.

Spencer, M. B., Dobbs, B., & Swanson, D. P. (1988). African American adolescents: Adaptational processes and socioeconomic diversity in behavioral outcomes. *Journal of Adolescence, 11,* 117-137.

Spencer, M. B., & Horowitz, F. D. (1973). Effects of systematic social and token reinforcement on the modification of racial and color concept attitudes in black and in white preschool children. *Developmental Psychology, 9,* 246-254.

Spencer, M. B., & Markstrom-Adams, C. (1990). Identity processes among racial and ethnic minority children in America. *Child Development, 61,* 290-310.

Stack, C. (1996). *Call to home.* New York: Basic Books.

Staines, G. L., & Pleck, J. H. (1983). *The impact of work schedules on the family.* Ann Arbor: University of Michigan Press.

Staples, R. (1981). *The world of black singles.* Westport, CT: Greenwood.

Staples, R. (Ed.). (1994). *The black family: Essays and studies* (5th ed.). Belmont, CA: Wadsworth.

Staples, R., & Johnson, L. (1993). *Black families at the crossroads.* San Francisco: Jossey-Bass.

Staples, R., & Mirande, A. (1980). Racial and cultural variations among American families: A decennial review of the literature on minority families. *Journal of Marriage and the Family, 40,* 157-173.

Stephens, T. D. (1985). Fixed sequence and circular-causal models of relationship development: Divergent views on the role of communication in intimacy. *Journal of Marriage and the Family, 47,* 955-963.

Stinnett, N. (1980). *Family strengths: Models for family life.* Lincoln: University of Nebraska Press.

Stinnett, N. (1981). In search of strong families. In N. Stinnett et al. (Eds.), *Building family strengths.* Lincoln: University of Nebraska Press.

Stinnett, N. (1983). Strong families. In D. Mace (Ed.), *Prevention in family services.* Beverly Hills, CA: Sage.

Tayeb, M. H. (1996). *The management of a multicultural workplace*. Chichester, New York: John Wiley.

Taylor, R. J. (1990). Need for support and family involvement among black Americans. *Journal of Marriage and the Family, 52*, 584-590.

Taylor, R. J., Chatters, L. M., & Mays, V. M. (1988). Parents, children, siblings, in-laws, and nonkin as sources of emergency assistance to black Americans. *Family Relations, 37*, 298-304.

Taylor, R. J., Chatters, L. M., Tucker, M. B., & Lewis, E. (1990). Developments in research on black families: A decade review. *Journal of Marriage and the Family, 52*, 993-1014.

Taylor, R. J., Leashore, B. R., & Toliver, S. (1988). An assessment of the provider role as perceived by black males. *Family Relations, 37*, 426-431.

Toliver, S. D. (1982). *The black family in slavery, the foundation of Afro American culture: Its importance to members of the slave community*. Unpublished doctoral dissertation, University of California, Berkeley.

Toliver, S. D. (1986). 20/20 vision: A perspective on women's changing roles and the structure of American families, past and future. *Frontiers, 9*(1), 27-31.

Tolson, T. F. J. (1990). The impact of two- and three-generational black family structure on perceived family climate. *Child Development, 61*, 416-428.

Tonnies, F. (1957). *Community and society*. East Lansing: Michigan State University Press. (Original work published in 1887)

Turner, R. D. (1985). The resurgence of racism on white campuses. *Black Collegian, 5*, 18-24.

Upson, N. (1974). *How to survive as a corporate wife*. New York: Doubleday.

Vance, B. (1989). *Planning and conducting family cluster*. Newbury Park, CA: Sage.

Vandervelde, M. (1979). *The changing life of the corporate wife*. New York: Mecox.

Veevers, J. E. (1973). Voluntary childless wives: An exploratory study. *Sociology and Social Research, April*, 356-365.

Visher, E., & Visher, J. (1983). Stepparenting: Blending families. In H. McCubbin & C. Figley (Eds.), *Stress and the family* (Vol. 1, pp. 133-146). New York: Brunner/Mazel.

Volling, B., & Belsky, J. (1991). Multiple determinants of father involvement during infancy in dual-earner and single-earner families. *Journal of Marriage and the Family, 53*, 461-474.

Voydanoff, P. (1980). Work roles as stressors in corporate families. *Family Relations, 29*, 489-494.

Voydanoff, P. (1984). *Work and family: Changing roles of men and women*. Palo Alto, CA: Mayfield.

Voydanoff, P., & Kelly, R. F. (1984). Determinants of work-related family problems among employed parents. *Journal of Marriage and the Family, 46*, 881-892.

Walsh, R. (1982). *Normal family process*. New York: Guilford.

Warshaw, L. (1979). *Managing stress*. Reading, MA: Addison-Wesley.

Washington, V. (1988). *Black children and American institutions: An ecological review and resource guide*. New York: Garland.

Washington, V., & La Point, V. (1987). *The cultural foundations of black children: Social status, public policy, and future directions*. New York: Garland.

Watson, M. F. (1988). Black adolescent identity development: Effects of perceived family structure. *Family Relations, 37*, 288-292.

Whyte, W. H. (1951a, October). The wives of management. *Fortune*, p. 86.

Whyte, W. H. (1951b, November). The corporation and the wife. *Fortune*, p. 109.

Wilkinson, D. Y. (1978). Toward a positive frame of references for analysis of black families. *Journal of Marriage and the Family, 40,* 707.

Willie, C. (1978). The inclining significance of race. *Society, 15,* 393-398.

Willie, C. (1979). *Caste and class controversy.* Dix Hills, NY: General Hall.

Willie, C. (1988). *A new look at black families.* Dix Hills, NY: General Hall.

Willie, C. (1989a). *Caste and class controversy on race and poverty.* Dix Hills, NY: General Hall.

Willie, C. (1989b). Child development in the context of the black extended family. *American Psychologist, 44,* 380-385.

Willie, C. (1991a). *Black and white families.* Dix Hills, NY: General Hall.

Willie, C. (1991b). *A new look at black families* (2nd ed.). Dix Hills, NY: General Hall.

Wilson, W. J. (1978a). *The declining significance of race.* Chicago: University of Chicago Press.

Wilson, W. J. (1978b). The declining significance of race. *Society, 15,* 385-392.

Wilson, W. J. (1978c). The declining significance of race: Revisited but not revised. *Society, 15*(5), 11-21.

Winett, R. A., & Neale, M. S. (1981). Flexible work schedules and family time allocation: Assessment of a system change on individual behavior using self-report logs. *Journal of Applied Behavior Analysis, 14*(1), 39-46.

Wyse, L. (1970). *Mrs. Success.* New York: World.

Yetman, N. R., & Steele, C. H. (1985). *Majority and minority.* Boston: Allyn & Bacon.

Zedeck, S. (1992). Exploring the domain of work and family concerns. In S. Zedeck (Ed.), *Work, families, and organizations* (pp. 1-32). San Francisco: Jossey-Bass.

Zinn, M. B., & Eitzen, D. S. (1987). *Diversity in American families.* New York: Harper & Row.

Zvonkovic, A. M., Greaves, K. M., Schmiege, C. J., & Hall, L. D. (1996). The marital construction of gender through work and family decisions: A qualitative analysis. *Journal of Marriage and the Family, 58*(1), 91-100.

Index

About the Author

Susan D. Toliver, Ph.D., is Associate Professor of Sociology and Director of Women's Studies at Iona College in New Rochelle, New York, where she previously held the position of Coordinator of Peace and Justice Education. She holds a doctoral degree in sociology from the University of California at Berkeley, and a master's degree in higher education administration from the University of Maryland, College Park. Her areas of specialization include the family, race and ethnic relations, and sex and gender studies. She has written about and researched the family, particularly the African American family. She is a member of several professional associations and is a past president of the New York State Council on Family Relations. At present, she serves as a member of the Advisory Council of the Connecticut Permanent Commission on the Status of Women. She has done extensive work in multiculturalism—directing faculty development activities; leading workshops; conducting seminars; and evaluating departmental, multi-institutional, and state-wide multicultural diversity projects. She is an AIDS activist and has conducted seminars and workshops on the subject as well as developed AIDS educational outreach materials for African American women.